Call Me Adam

SECOND EDITION

❧✦☙

Je suis stupide, Je suis laid, J'ai faim,
I'm stupid, I'm ugly, I'm hungry

A truly Canadian novel
Based on the Rag to Riches story of Arthur Adam
As told to a Ghostwriter

❧✦☙

ARTHUR ADAM

Arthur Adam

Call Me Adam: First Edition Copywrite © 2015

SECOND EDITION
Copyright © 2020 Arthur Adam
All rights reserved.

This is a work of creative nonfiction. The events are portrayed to the best of Arthur Adam's memory. While all the stories in this book are true, some names and identifying details have been changed to protect the privacy of the people involved.

Published by Arthur Adam, 2020

Layout, design, and cover by Marianne Curtis
emeraldpublication@gmail.com
Printed by Createspace

Published in Canada

Archives Canada
ISBN-13: 979-8577155636

DEDICATION

This book is dedicated to my wife - without her help I could not have done this book, to my siblings - because they are part of me and to "overcomers" in life - that could be you.

CONTENTS

	Introduction	i
	Foreword	iii
	The Trail – Part One	1
1	Joe and Berthe	3
2	Arthur - Five Years Later	11
3	School	19
4	Spelling	23
5	Stuttering	27
6	Altar Boys	31
7	Money	35
	The Trail – Part Two	43
8	The Finger	47
9	The Cookies	53
10	The Peanut	55
11	The Watch	59
12	The Truck	63
13	Food	67
14	Church	71
15	The Beating	75
	The Trail – Part Three	79
16	The Bunker	83

17	Chores	87
18	Changes	93
19	The Fight	95
	The Trail – Part Four	99
20	Kicked Out	103
21	The Kindness of Strangers	109
22	St. Boniface	113
23	The Search for Theresa	117
24	Jim	121
25	Driver's License	125
26	Parents Love Their Children	129
27	Newdale Construction	131
	The Trail – Part Five	139
28	Deer Hunting in Winnipeg	145
29	A Hard Lesson	151
30	Starting Over	153
31	The Patent	157
32	Levelling Out the Playing Field	161
	The Trail – Part Six	167
	The Final Word	171
	About the Author	179

ACKNOWLEDGMENTS

I would like to thank Norbert, who spoke willingly and passionately about his early life with honesty and integrity. Most of my siblings call themselves Adams not Adam.

A word about my mama. My mama hated me and watched me twenty-four seven. She always said she had a problem, I was that problem, but she was a good woman. Before she died, she asked for forgiveness for the things she had done to me. Me, I loved my mama.

This book is meant as a memoir, not a book of historical facts. The happenings, stories, and memories belong to Arthur Adam.

INTRODUCTION

BY A GHOST WRITER

Call Me Adam…

"I went to the newspaper, eh?" He said over the telephone. "I told the editor I was looking for a writer who could write a book about me. He gave me your name and number and said you were the only one he knew who could do this."

"Look for a tall Frenchman," he said. I laughed. We were meeting in the French Canadian town of La Broquerie, Manitoba.

I entered the hotel café the next day and directly across from me, blocking the entrance to the formal dining room, was a man sitting at a table. He stared at me as if I were the prey and he the hunter. His name was Arthur Adam.

"Call me Adam," he said as he moved the table back into its original corner. I took the chair facing him. We were alone in the large dining room with 135 empty chairs. Everyone else, it seemed, chose to give us our privacy and eat their lunch in the overcrowded booths of the connected café.

Adam, tall and stocky, was about 60-years-old. His white shirt was accompanied by dark dress pants. The black curls on his head were helped and flipped to one side and then swooped, hinting at a duck-tail. The two top buttons on his shirt were open, exposing a gold chain, and I thought I smelled Aqua Velva. He wore a ring on the index finger of his left hand—a flash of diamonds and gold—a ring that could do damage to a man's face in a dark alley or used as a down-payment on a house.

With rough and calloused fingers Adam fiddled with the cutlery on the table and then laid his hands flat, palms down, on either side of the place setting. He leaned forward. His look was careful as he tried to hide his struggle between indecision and purpose. I sensed power—and a story.

"Okay—I was raised in the bush, me," Adam began. "In a place called St. Labre, Manitoba. It's close to the US border, but so poor the Americans don't want it and so far into the bush the rest of Canada don't know it's there. I'm the middle kid of 19 kids. We had no bathroom: no outhouse, no beds. I always ducked when my dad walked past in case he'd hit me. I have a grade 2 education; can't read or write.

I had no English, only poor French when I was kicked out of the house at 15-years-old." (He paused.)

"I was on my way to making my first million dollars."

"Okay—you write my story?"

❧ ❖ ☙

Okay. Here is his story…

FOREWORD

Yesterday I was at Shiloh—that's the name I gave the place where I grew up. It's all fixed up now, with a new house standing on the very spot the old shack stood. Everything is clean; trees planted everywhere, a woodshed and old farm machinery around on the grass. It's peaceful now. Still, the memories are there, but I am different. While I have forgiveness in my heart for the way I grew up, it doesn't mean I have forgotten. I cannot forget. It's inside me still.

I look at the yard where things happened. I got such sad memories. I grew up in fear—fear and hunger. I was kicked out of the house at fifteen with only a grade two education. I couldn't read or write. I only spoke poor French and all I owned was the clothes on my back. Leaving home and the choices after that, okay—it was tough. But it changed my life. I don't know what would have happened to me if I hadn't been thrown out that young. I do know one thing. If I had stayed and lived that way for the rest of my life—I would wish to have never been born. To never exist is better than the way I lived. It was just hell on earth. It was that awful. My brothers and sisters maybe have a different story—some better—some worse. But for me it was nothing to be remembered in fondness. There was nothing good that was there.

The best thing that happened to me in my life was getting kicked out of that shack in the bush. A few years later, I was on my way to becoming a millionaire.

This is my story…

The old homestead in St. Labre as it appears today.

"I never wanted to be taken by money, but when it came, it sure felt good. Okay—I never wanted to think I was something that I'm not. But in the meanwhile, when the money did come, it was a heck of a good feeling."

—Arthur Adam

PART ONE

THE TRAIL

Son, you know it's cold when the sap freezes so hard the trees crack open with a loud pop. In the dark, in the bush, it sounds like a boot stepping on wood, eh? You don't notice it unless you're alone. And if you're alone in the bush because you're a bonehead, that pop sounds like a gunshot and almost makes you shit your britches. You jump. Your heart races hoping there is someone there; someone to help. You wait and listen, Son. There is another pop farther away. You know then it's just the trees and your heart beats back to normal and the cold seems colder and the darkness blacker.

Eh Boy! And so here I am, alone with my stupidity.

Okay—I know the bush, eh? Son, I was raised in the bush. I know trouble in the bush. In the bush, Son, you don't fool around. I know that. I was filled with fear all my life, about the bush.

In summertime, I do my construction. From Christmas time to March or April, we don't do construction because it's too cold when the ground is frozen. The winters in Manitoba are just brutal out in the open like that. I never do construction jobs in the winter unless it pays an arm and a leg. But I can't sit around. Okay—I need to be always busy, me. Always I'm moving—can't sit still. Never could.

This time, Son, I talk my brother, your Uncle Leo, into coming and working at a bush camp near Bissette cutting and hauling logs. We don't need to be there until Monday morning, but we decide to leave tonight—Sunday night.

Okay—I decide we're going to the camp tonight.

We haven't been to this camp before, so we really don't know how to find it when we get to the bush road. In the bush there aren't any road signs. The roads are only a trail cut in; and private. You don't even need a license to drive your car on them and no speed limit. See? Not really roads at all. They're not on maps and no paving or nothing. Truck tracks through the bushes, some of them. Just the tire tracks of the last truck through and that's it.

Well, it had snowed a lot for a few days and then it was very cold—very cold. We left Winnipeg at about 7 o'clock at night and headed to Bissette about hundred and twenty miles away. About thirty-five miles past Bissette, we turn onto a little bush road, following directions we got from the foreman. The bush road is closed to the public. It's only an access road to the camps and nowhere else, and we keep driving maybe another twenty miles.

Joe and Berthe raise 19 children in this tiny little house in St. Labre.

CHAPTER ONE

JOE AND BERTHE

Joseph Adam (Joe) was born December 28th, 1905 in Maskinongé, Quebec, one of six children to George Adam and Armidas Sarrasin. His father, a fisherman, died from the Spanish flu that swept across Canada after the First Great War in 1918. Joe was thirteen when his father died. He had three older sisters, who he couldn't get along with and left home at the age of fourteen with a loaf of bread under his arm. He didn't have a clue where he was going.

Joe rode the freight trains looking for work. His travels took him to Rhode Island, St. Jean Baptiste and then landed him in Carrick, Manitoba at the age of twenty-seven. It was the Great Depression and the Manitoba government was shipping young men out of the cities and into bush camps. The men received room and board and a small amount of money per month. They cut white spruce and balsam and, in the Spring, they planted trees. It was the only way to make any money—working in the bush—unless you were hired on by the Manitoba Dairy Farms in Marchand. Farm hands were subsidized by the government as well. It was tough times for everyone.

There wasn't much to do for entertainment back then, mostly

church dances and church socials. Joe was a good dancer and Carrick and Woodridge were nearby towns. People from all the neighboring towns would go to the same dances.

Berthe Yvonne Marie Gauthier was born on June 25, 1919 in Warroad, Minnesota, U.S.A. She was one of six children born to Édouard Gauthier and Hermina Grenier. The family spent their early years in Alberta before moving to Woodridge, Manitoba where her father sought employment with the railroad. They later moved to the small town of St. Labre.

Joe met two of Berthe's sisters at a dance. Later he was doing road work close to Berthe's house and her sisters recognized him from the dance. They made Berthe go out and talk to him. The attraction was fast and mutual. After a very short courtship, they were married on July 27, 1935. Joe was twenty-eight and Berthe had turned sixteen a month earlier. The only promise Joe made to Berthe on their wedding day was that she would always have good water and a lot of wood to burn in the stove. He was a hard man!

The newlyweds moved into a house Joe built about two miles from St. Labre. It wasn't much to look at, but it was theirs. Joe used to say the room was so small, they had to sleep one on top of the other. The main floor was wide open with the ceiling held up by posts. There was one room upstairs without a door so the heat from the wood stoves on the main floor could rise and heat the upstairs. When their tenth child, Arthur, was twelve-years-old, they built a new house with four bedrooms upstairs.

Joe was known in town as Tiger because of his strictness, hard as nails attitude and roaring personality. He was tall, over six feet, with dark hair and eyes. He was not easily influenced and was very vocal about his opinions which, didn't always sit well with the other townspeople. He was a great storyteller, when he was in the mood. When he started telling a story people would crowd around him to listen—which was often. Outside church, there would often be a crowd gathering with Joe in the middle, waving arms and keeping everyone mesmerized.

On their acres, the Adams started farming. Joe earned money by selling firewood or fence posts he'd cut and haul out of the bush. He was, however, well-known for his tracking abilities and his trapping.

"You living the life of a bum, you—trapping," a neighbor once told him as he watched Joe skinning his day's catch.

"How much money did you make today?" Joe asked him.

"Well," he said, "I made my two cords of wood today, so that's $6."

"I cut a cord of wood today," Joe said. "But here I also caught a mink—$24. And then look—here's another mink. Here's a beaver $18 and here are some weasels a buck a piece. So," He stood up and looked the man in the eyes, "Who's the bum?"

It was three years after their marriage, before Berthe became pregnant. After the first child was born, a daughter, she gave birth almost every year until the two had a family of thirteen boys and six girls.

When Joe worked in the bush, Berthe went with him. Sometimes it was cutting and splitting firewood for themselves and for sale. Other times it was cutting fence posts for sale. This work meant Berthe had to use a planer and peel the bark off the newly cut logs. Her hands were small and not as strong as Joe's and he'd get frustrated.

"You're doing it wrong!" He'd yell as he always did, to her or any kid. He would threaten them, call them names, run them down, belittle them, til they would feel like crap. That's how Joe Adam dealt with his family.

Once, Joe and Berthe were out in the woods, cutting trees for the woodstoves. As usual, he was not happy with Berthe's performance and a neighbor who was also working in the woods heard Joe say: "If you don't do better than that, I'll throw the axe at you." The neighbor immediately ran to Joe and told him if he did that, he would have to deal with him. Joe stopped his bitching instantly.

After their third child things became financially difficult for the couple and Joe counted every penny, and every scrap of food. He demanded the cows, pigs and chickens were well looked after. They were all they had to eat and what was left over they sold. He cared more for this pigs and cows than his kids who were there for him to use and abuse.

"Berthe!" Joe yelled when he came in one day, "Did you feed those chickens?"

"Yes, Joe. I feed the chickens every day."

Joe went stomping out to the coop and grabbed a chicken by the throat. Checking the gullet, he saw it empty of grain.

"You did NOT feed them!" he yelled at her as he stormed into the house. He hit Berthe, yelling and swearing at her. Terrified, she ran out of the house, leaving the children behind, running most of the way to her mother's house in town.

After calming down, she started worrying about the children. She didn't think Joe would hurt them, but then she didn't think he would hurt her either. Then Joe arrived on the doorstep.

Joe talked to Berthe's mother first. "Forgive me," he said to her. "I don't know what happened, but I promise you, it will never happen again. Tell Berthe to come home. The children need her."

Berthe went to the church to speak to the Priest. She was bruised, but the wounds were mostly on the inside. She was obviously frightened.

Joe had already come into town and spoken to the priest, so the Father knew what happened.

"Father, Joe wants me to go back home. I'm afraid," Berthe told the priest.

"You took the vows of marriage, Berthe. Those are sacred vows. The church does not recognize divorce."

"But Father, what if he continues to hit me?"

"You have children—you are a mother and a wife. Your duty is to your husband."

Berthe went back to her husband. Joe was relieved. He couldn't look after kids and work the farm on his own, it was too hard.

Berthe followed the advice of the Church. She never stood up for herself after that. Never again would she rise against her husband. She became the faithful wife, the abused wife who never answered back for fear he would hit her again. She became very religious, and prayed a lot. If only she had stood up to Joe, he would have stopped hitting her. Deep down, he was scared of losing her. Berthe did not realize the power she had on her husband.

Joe kept his promise—as far as he was concerned. He still slapped her on occasion, but he never lost control.

His promise never included his children, however.

"There's a cow out there yelling Berthe," yelled Joe from his chair. The radio was on and the cow was drowning out Tennessee Ernie Ford. Joe was rolling smokes. The older kids were all in school, only the three little ones were at home.

"I hear it Joe, I'm going out there right now. And don't yell like that, the kids are sleeping," Berthe walked past him towards the door. He smiled as she passed. She was seven months pregnant with number twelve and he knew it was a boy. She always waddled like that when she carried a boy. That would be good. Another boy to help him run the farm since the others were growing up and leaving home.

"I just have to bring in some firewood first or I won't be able to bake bread today and we'll run out and the kids need lunches for school tomorrow. I'll see to the cow after the wood."

"For Christ sake hurry up." Joe picked up his tobacco tin and put a cigarette in his mouth. He grabbed some more papers and kept rolling while he watched Berthe waddle over to the wood pile and lift four or five good sized logs into her tiny arms. He marveled at how strong she was for such a little girl—only five foot two.

Berthe struggled to open the door with her arms full of wood. She kicked off her boots and carried the wood over to the wood box by the cook stove. Joe watched and licked the paper on another cigarette as she put her boots back on before going to the barn to see about the bellowing cow.

"You're going to need more wood than that," said Joe. "And get the cows some water."

"I'll bring in some more right after I see to the cows," she said as she closed the door behind her.

Joe grabbed another paper and a pinch of tobacco between three fingers. Spreading it just right, he started to roll another cigarette when he saw a cow come out of the barn with Berthe waddling behind it. He licked the paper and smiled—another smoke done. Joe looked out the window again as he reached for another paper. Berthe wasn't there. He sighed.

'Hope she hurries up,' he thought to himself. *'I could use a cup of tea.'*

Joe rolled another smoke, but no Berthe. Now he was getting angry. *'What the hell is that lazy woman doing out there? She said she had to bake bread.'*

"Berthe," Joe yelled as he got up from his chair. He stomped over and opened the door. "Berthe! What are you wasting time with now? You said you were going to make bread."

Joe stops dead. Berthe is laying in the yard and there's blood running down her legs. She's crying and holding on to her stomach.

"It's too early, Joe," she said. "Get the midwife."

❧ ❖ ☙

Two-year-old Arthur heard his Mama's screams. He was scared. He was upstairs with his brothers and sisters. The midwife told them all to stay there until she came and got them. But it had been so long and Arthur wanted his Mama.

Creeping to the stairs, the toddler sat on his bum and slid down a step at a time until he could see Mama and Papa's bed under the stairwell. Mama looked awful—there was blood everywhere and she was sobbing. The midwife held a tiny little baby in one hand as she wiped him down with a rag. Arthur thought he looked funny, so small with spider legs and arms.

Joseph, they named him. He was so small. When he cried, it sounded like a kitten meowing. At first, he seemed to grow, but at two-and-a-half months Berthe and Joe took him to St. Boniface Hospital in Winnipeg because he had started losing weight. Berthe had been feeding him eight ounces of water, eight ounces of canned milk and four tablespoons of corn syrup a day. She started adding a bit of pablum because he was losing weight.

The nurses weighed and measured him at the hospital. He weighed three pounds and four ounces and was thirteen-inches long. The doctors couldn't believe he had survived.

Joseph grew into a young man, without malice, a bit slow, but he helped his dad around the farm, with the chores, cutting wood and any other chores Joe would give him. Later, he lived with his sister Mona and spent time working at Kindale, in Steinbach, where he passed away in 2019. Everybody loved him, he forever said: "I pray for you" and was always willing to help others.

Many years later, once Arthur had built his camp at "Shiloh" on the old homestead, he bought a quad for Joseph so he could come and give rides to some of his friends. Joseph loved to give them rides around the old homestead. He had a big heart and Arthur loved him very much.

Arthur used to go to Texas in the wintertime, and Joseph always knew that when the geese were gathering to fly south, Arthur would be leaving too. That made Joseph sad. But, when he saw the first geese appear in the Spring, he would get all excited and say things like: "Is Arthur back? I just saw the geese today." He was always excited to see Arthur again and spend some time on the old farm once more.

When Berthe became older, Joseph loved to look after her. He adored the car rides, and would always sit his mother in the front seat and he would sit in the back seat right behind her. It was very important to him to be seated right behind her. No one else could have that seat. When Berthe became ill, Mona would look after Joseph. He had a hard time understanding why his mother was not coming home. When she passed away in 2009, his sister couldn't tell him that she was gone, for the longest time. Joseph would always ask why he could not visit his mother and never understood why the doctors were not able to heal her. Finally, when he was told, he cried and cried. Joseph was a simple child in a man's body.

※

Go by your gut feeling.

CHAPTER TWO

ARTHUR - FIVE YEARS LATER

Heavy coats and blankets hide a mêlée of arms and legs. The pungent smell of sweat invades the little boy's nostrils. His hair—crisp with frost—sticks to his forehead. His eyes flutter open, taking revenge on his bone-weary body. He looks up at the light coming through the frost-speckled window in the roof's peak. It's the light of dawn.

"W-Why aren't there s-s-street lights in St. Labre," he asked his dad one evening in the nearby town of Steinbach.

"You idiot, Arthur," his dad cuffed him across the head. "Who puts street lights in the bush?"

Arthur's legs hurt. He wants to move but can't. There's a brother lying in front of him and one behind. He can't straighten his legs because theirs are bent too. If they lay with straightened legs their feet get cold because the coats covering them are too short. He sighs. He wants to sleep but his stomach is awake and he needs to pee. Chores are waiting. No breakfast until after the chores are done.

Turning over on the floor, he crawls out of the mass of humanity. He's still dressed from the day before and the day before that; perhaps a week before that. It's hard to do laundry in the winter and when most of the children only own one set of clothes—it's even harder.

A noise came from the girls sleeping under the window on the floor. His two older sisters are waking up and starting to move around. Mona is asleep on the floor by Berthe and Joe's bed downstairs. The main floor is one big room and the ceiling is held up by beams. The wood-burning cook-stove and the box stove stood against the wall. There was a wash stand next to the door with a wash bowl on top and a crap pail and a slop pail for the pigs underneath. The table stood on the other side of the door with a cream separator and a kneading counter for making bread. Around the table were benches and old chairs.

Arthur panics and races down the stairs. He really has to pee. Berthe is already in the kitchen when Arthur rushes to put on his boots, coat and toque; wiggling and hopping from foot to foot. Berthe has a baby on her hip and his oldest sister has another one in her arms as she helps Berthe make breakfast. In the corner by the door the wind is blowing through a crack in the wall and a small hill of snow is forming on the floor. Frost has painted the inside of the windows with snowflake-like designs, even though the big stove and the cook stove are both roaring.

Berthe is too busy to notice Arthur; as is his sister. Silently, he slips out the door as the rest of his brothers and sisters come down the stairs. The little ones will be peeing in the can at the front door, but Arthur's too old for that. He struggles through the snowdrifts covering the yard and goes into the barn. He relieves himself against the back wall. Oh, that wonderful feeling as he empties his bladder.

"B-b-better than sex," Arthur says to the cow next to him. He really doesn't know what that means—he's only eight—but his older brother says that all the time.

Arthur usually goes into the bush, but on really cold days like today the kids use the barn. There are two adults and fifteen kids in the family—almost sixteen. The bushes near the house grow tall and green. Arthur is happy he got to the barn first. He can't do his business if anyone else is there. He doesn't know why—he just can't. In a minute the older ones will all be in here finding their own corners of privacy, or they will brave the cold. The barn will get cleaned after milking, so whatever the kids do in the barn will get shoveled out with the cow manure.

It makes Arthur mad sometimes—or embarrassed—when he thinks about it. The school, the store and the church all have outhouses. So do his friends, his cousins and the neighbors—the whole damn town has outhouses. Joe built a place for the cows to go, but not his kids.

Arthur's stomach growls as he runs to the house to start his chores. Stepping through the door, he grabs the crap bucket with both hands. It's heavy and really full and the smell burns his nostrils. It's his turn to empty it.

"Ôte toé du chemin!" (Get out of my way) one of his brothers shoves him and Arthur falls against the wall. Using both hands, he lugs the pail sloshing and splashing out the door and into the bushes beside the house. Dropping the bucket on its side he holds his nose and watches as everything flows onto the clean white snow.

After returning the crap pail back into the house, Arthur has to get water for the cows. Fighting through the snow drifts Arthur makes his way to the second well, which is about 140 meters from the house. The wind has picked up and ice-crystals in the air sting his face. The other kids have let the cows out of the barn so they can clean it and the animals crowd around him as he picks up the waterbucket. The cows need water and the well close to the house has run dry. He hates this job and Joe knows it. Arthur can feel Joe's eyes on him. He knows that he is sitting in his chair by the window and watching to make sure the cows will get enough water.

There's no wooden crank—just a bucket on a frozen rope with loops stiff and cold and slippery. He hates this job worse than emptying the crap bucket even. The well has a layer of ice on it and he has to drop the bucket a few times before it breaks through and the bucket fills with water. He has mitts on and they slip on the icy rope. The rope arches stiffly behind him as he heaves up the bucket hand-over-fist. The bucket keeps catching on the wall of the well and he wiggles the rope to loosen it so it doesn't tip and spill and the rope—so slippery—slides through his frozen fingers and lands back at the bottom and he starts again. Getting it back to the top again, he steps on the rope to keep it tight while he reaches for the bucket with both hands and tries to lift it over the lip of the well.

His fingers are numb and clumsy and he spills almost half of the water down the front of his coat before he can get the bucket out of the well. He wants to cry. His gloves are also wet. And this is just the first bucket. The cows crowd around the trough and push Arthur as he fights to dump the bucket. Sticking their lips into the dribble of water in the bottom of the trough they suck up what's there. It's not enough. They stomp their feet and snort clouds of hot breath. Over and over, bucket by bucket, he hauls water for the cows. His arms ache. He keeps going. His fingers freeze and he pauses for a minute to warm them under his arms. He can't stop though; he knows Joe is still sitting in his chair and watching out the window. Joe doesn't care how hard it is, how cold it is, or how wet his clothes are. He only cares that the cows get water.

Finally done, cold, tired and hungry, Arthur drives the cows back into the warm barn. One of the nuns at school once told him she thought the smell of barns was warm and comforting. He smiled quietly as he thought of that. He doubted she has ever stepped foot in a real barn—to him the smell was cloying. It smelled of work.

After the chores are done the kids break the ice on the top of the wash bowl and try to scrub the barn off their fingers. They all use the same water, shaking their hands dry or wiping them on their clothes before migrating to the kitchen to wait by the table—circling and drooling.

They have to wait for Berthe to say they can sit down—bread, homemade butter, porridge, milk—it's all put on the table and his stomach turns over as his mouth waters. There are no eggs this morning. They only get the eggs that Berthe doesn't sell or need for baking and in the winter when it's this cold the chickens don't lay as much.

Berthe gives them a look and they sit down. Arthur sits next to Joe. Berthe gives Joe the most and whoever sits next to him has a chance to get what he leaves on his plate when he's had enough or if he's in a good mood he might toss someone an extra piece of toast.

Papa says grace, then everyone grabs for the food. Standing up Arthur snatches a piece of toast and sticks it on his plate as he grabs another piece in one hand and a bowl of porridge in the other. Before his bum is back on the chair, he has scooped up porridge with his toast and is in heaven as the warmth fills his mouth—he doesn't chew it, he just swallows that first bite. Sometimes there are lumps in the porridge and those lumps are hard to swallow without gagging. When that happens, Arthur breaks his bread into chunks and stirs it in with the porridge, so the lumps don't bother him—but not this morning. Berthe's porridge is smooth and thick. Within minutes, even the table is bare of crumbs. Arthur uses the last of his bread to wipe his porridge bowl clean and then he licks his fingers. His stomach still hurts, but there is nothing left; not even on Joe's plate. He looks around to see if anyone has food left over that he can eat. He catches Berthe's glare. He looks at Papa. He's lighting a cigarette. Berthe might give him some more to eat with Papa sitting there.

"C-can I have another t-toast, Mama?" He knows she doesn't want him to have one, even though there's more bread on the counter, "Or just a piece of b-bread?"

"No. You've had enough."

He can see she's mad at him for asking. He knows by the look she gives him that when Joe isn't around. He'll be in big trouble.

"I'm still hungry, Mama. There's b-bread on the counter, c-can't I please have a piece?" He's already in trouble; if he's going to be punished later, he might as well have a full stomach.

"Arthur! I told you no! You've had enough, now get to school." His dad stood up and grabbed a piece of bread and tossed it on the table in front of her.

"Tabarnak! Make him some toast. The boy is hungry."

Berthe was so angry she made Arthur three huge pieces of toast and he had to eat them or he would have been in even more trouble.

'Okay—I'm happy,' he smiles to himself.

After eating his toast Arthur runs upstairs to get his school books. Downstairs he can hear one of his older brothers talking with Berthe.

"Why do you hate Arthur?" he asks.

"Time for school," she says.

"Mama, why? He's just a little boy."

"I don't hate him, he's a bad kid. I'm trying to teach him."

"Mama, you are harder on him than on anyone. You do hate him. I see it."

Arthur gulps back tears. He wants to cry, but he can't cry here. His brothers and sisters will see him and he'd have to tell them something. What could he say?

"I'm crying because Mama hates me and I feel lonely inside, even though I'm in this large family?" They would all laugh at him. Besides, he always knew Berthe had a fault—he was her fault.

'So, what if Mama hates me,' he thought. 'I'm almost grown up. It doesn't matter.'

Arthur grabs his lunch and waits for his younger sister, Lynne. She's a year younger, but tiny and has pink rubber boots she wears everywhere. Arthur carries both their books and lunches and lets her grab the back of his coat as he runs. Her little boots are like skis, sliding on the hard snow. He pulls her across the field until her little fingers get tired and can't hold on anymore. She's only got a thin little coat. He opens his and wraps it around her so they can share its warmth while they walk. The school is about three and a half kilometers away if you go by the road, but closer through the bush. It's so cold this morning dad said to leave the cows in the barn; but the kids have to walk to school no matter how cold it is, unless the Priest, Father Giroux, comes by and gives them a ride—but not this morning. This morning they are on their own.

Two kilometers from home lived Godmother Marie Ange Grenier. She is the sweetest lady and everyone loves her so much. Arthur and his sister were so cold they knocked on her door to see if they could come in to warm up.

"Come in, come in," she pushes them close to the wood stove. Slipping off his sister's jacket, Marie Ange gets a needle and thread and sews on a button while they get warm. Her own daughter had already left for school.

The town of St. Labre is tiny. Arthur's family is related to almost everyone on his mother's side. The schoolhouse is in town, across the road from the Church. On one side of the church, just a little behind it, is the cemetery inside a fence with a gate along the front. On the other side of the church is the convent where five nuns live. Next to the convent is the store. That is the town of St. Labre.

❧ ❖ ☙

Own your own mistakes. Don't blame someone else.

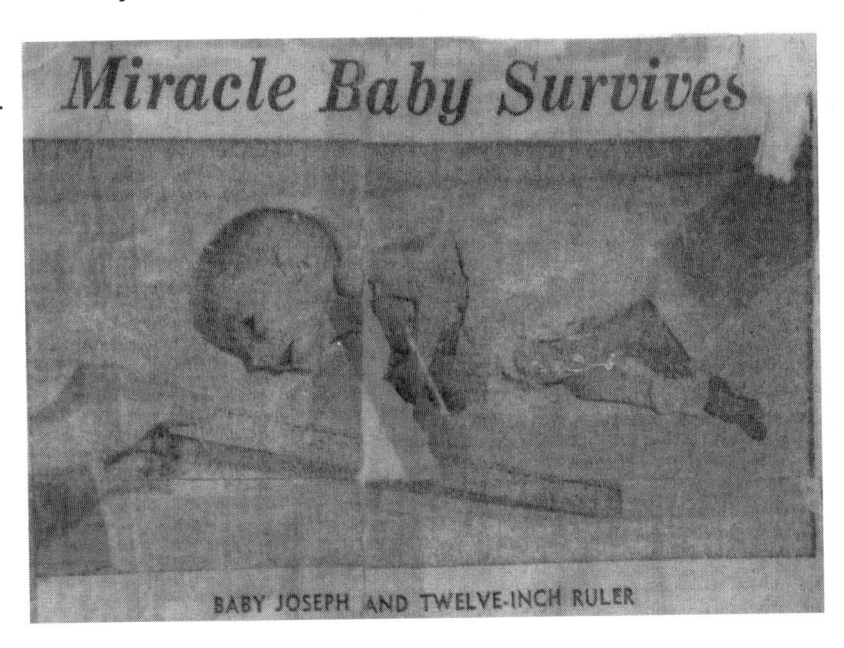

Joseph's delivery made the local news.

Arthur as a little boy on the farm.

CHAPTER THREE

SCHOOL

The old wooden schoolhouse looks forlorn against the grey sky this morning. The trees surrounding it, bare of leaves, appear dead. Snow was piled high where the caretaker of the church, who also shoveled and cleared the paths to the school, had pushed the windblown flakes. Out of the chimney curled a steady stream. The playground, littered with snow forts and snowmen, was empty of children. The Adam kids were the last to arrive.

Arthur and his sister climbed the steps and hung their coats in the hall. They snuck into their seats quietly, hoping the sister wouldn't notice they were late. She noticed. But she decided to ignore it since it was only a couple of minutes.

Arthur and his sister were in the same room, the older grades were downstairs in the other room. Although Arthur was eight, he was still in Grade one. He still can't read or write.

His first day of school had been exciting. He had looked forward to learning to read and being a big kid, not staying home with Berthe like the babies.

"Just look at those curls," the Sister had said to him as she ran her fingers through his dark hair. He looked up at her and smiled.

'Okay—she likes me,' he thought to himself.

"Am I good lookin'?" he had asked her. "Am I maybe the b-b-best lookin' one in the s-s-school?"

The Sister's face changed from soft to hard.

"No," she said abruptly. "You are the ugliest kid in the class. Take your seat." And from there his experience in school was all downhill.

"Everyone," said the Sister, "Get out your spelling books." There was a shuffling of papers and everyone except for Arthur pulled out his book.

"Arthur," the Sister stood over him. "Where is your spelling?"

"You never g-give me one so I don't got n-n-none," he said.

"Did you bring money for the spelling book? You have to buy them, they aren't free."

"N-n-no M-ma'am," a few kids snickered while he struggled to talk. "I ain't got money and Papa n-n-never give me any," he could feel his face get hot.

"After school today, you go home and tell your Papa the spelling book cost fifty cents and bring me the money tomorrow. The books aren't free."

Arthur didn't really care about not having books. If he didn't have the books, then he wouldn't have to do homework, which was just fine.

"Look at someone else's. Bring your money tomorrow."

The morning passed slowly. Arthur was getting hungry. He ate half his lunch at recess, although it was awful. Two pieces of bread spread with lard. He scraped off all the lard he could and then ate one of the pieces, saving the other one for lunch.

Everyone was to remain in their chairs when they ate lunch. This was the worst time for Arthur. At recess, he could hide what he ate, but it was really hard to hide his lunch when everyone was there.

"Yuk, Arthur what is that on your bread?"

"It's fat," he folded the bread so it didn't show. "Mama says I'm not b-b-big enough so she puts it on my b-b-bread to make me grow-up with really b-b-big muscles." His big brother, Norbert looked at him from across the room. He was only a year older and in grade four. He was not only Arthur's brother, he was his best friend. Norbert smiled and so did Arthur. Arthur knew Norbert was laughing at his stutter, and that was okay.

Arthur ate his bread as fast as he could and then sat there and waited. One by one the kids finished their lunches and went outside to play, leaving their lunch boxes under their chairs. Still Arthur waited. A couple of kids threw some bread crusts in the garbage and an apple core. Arthur waited and pretended to be chewing. Finally, the Sister and all the kids had left, leaving him the only one in the room. He walked over to the garbage and pulled out the sandwich crusts. They had peanut butter on them. He ate them and oh, they tasted like heaven. The apple core was next and then he ate a banana peel. There was nothing left in the garbage so he checked the desks before going outside to play like the others.

After school the kids finished their chores early and played hide and seek upstairs. Arthur was looking for a place to hide. The walls upstairs in the bedrooms were sloped to follow the peak. Arthur crawled through a hole in the wall into the rafters and found a bunch of rags with blood all over them. He didn't know what they were and was really scared. He thought someone was hurt and ran downstairs to show Berthe.

"Mom! Mom! Look—I found these upstairs," he held them up for her to look at.

"You dirty boy," she yelled at him, "You dirty, dirty boy. You get back upstairs and you keep out of things that have nothing to do with you." Berthe grabbed the rags and threw them into the fire.

Arthur didn't know why his Mama was upset, but he must have done something wrong. He just didn't know what.

☙❖☙

It costs a lot of money to be a showoff.

CHAPTER FOUR

SPELLING

"Papa," Arthur said after supper that night, "I need to bring fifty cents to the school for a spelling book. The nun told me to tell you."

"Ah! Chalice!" Joe's fist came down on the table. Berthe gave him a look. "What is it with these Nuns? They always want something. School is good for nothing. It's stupid and the lazy Nuns, they don't know nothing and they all want money. The other kids, they got the spelling book for free. You go back to school tomorrow and you tell her, Arthur. The spelling books are free and I'm not giving you nothing. You go and tell the nun the spelling books are free and I ain't giving you spit. You tell that nun; she is going to hell."

Arthur went to school the next day and when he was asked for the fifty cents to pay for the spelling, he told the nun.

"M-m-my Papa s-s-said he's not g-giving you s-s-spit. They are free," some of the kids snickered and then the room went silent. They watched the sister to see what she would do. She stared at Arthur.

"I don't think your Papa said that."

"He d-d-did say that."

"I think you took the fifty cents your Papa gave you for the spelling book and spent it on candy."

The nun grabbed him and made him put on his coat. She marched him outside to the north side of the school house and turned him around to face the wind blowing snow in gusts at the side of the school building. It was the middle of winter and really cold. He didn't have gloves or a hat, just a thin coat and usually no underclothes. The wind drove the cold right into his bones.

"You will have to stand here like this whenever we do work in our spelling books," she shook her finger in his face. "and during every recess and every lunch and for fifteen minutes at three o'clock before you go home until you bring fifty cents for a spelling book."

Arthur stood there for the rest of the morning and the nun poked her head out the window to make sure he stayed where she put him. The north wind battered his face and thin little coat with snow—but he didn't move. He wouldn't give the nun that satisfaction. He would show her how tough an Adam he was.

After school Arthur told his dad what happened and Joe was angry.

"That nun has the devil in her," he yelled. "I don't care what she does I am not paying fifty cents for a free spelling book. She will not blackmail me."

Arthur didn't tell the nun exactly what Joe had said. He simply continued to stand outside for most of the morning, and after lunch and during recess and again at three o'clock.

He was miserable. He was so cold at the end of the day he was shaking when she let him back into the warm classroom.

Day after frigid day he continued to stand outside and face the north wind. All month his dad yelled and every day the nun yelled and Arthur continued to freeze.

Joe went into the town of Woodridge on his monthly trip, to sell wood. He went and spoke to the nun at the school there and asked her how much the spelling books cost. The nun looked at him funny.

"Why, Mr. Adam. The spelling books are free." And she gave him one for Arthur.

At school on Tuesday the nun told the class to take out their spelling books and open them. She saw Arthur sitting in his desk and looked really mad.

"Arthur, did you bring your fifty cents?"

"No, Sister."

"Then get outside and stand on the north wall while we do our lesson."

"No Ma'am," he said. "My Papa said I d-d-didn't have to do that no more."

"Your Papa does not teach this class—I do. I'm telling you that until you bring me fifty cents for a spelling book you will stand outside."

"Okay," he said and tried not to smile. "But Papa w-won't like it, since he went to Woodridge where the n-n-nun there gave him a spelling book and said the spelling b-b-books are free," And Arthur took out his spelling book and put it on his desk, opening it up to the correct page. Then he looked up at the nun. He never remembered seeing anyone change all those colors before. Her mouth moved but she didn't say anything and he never went outside again to stand facing north.

Papa won that one, but the nun wasn't through with him yet. There was an all-out feud between the Sister and Joe after that, and Arthur was caught in the middle so he was the one who had to pay with the punishment. The nun kept her eye on him, the same way his mom watched him. She wanted to catch him doing something wrong and he was very careful not to let that happen. His being good didn't help; she was getting angrier as time went on.

❧❖❦

What I regret the most are the things I didn't do.

CHAPTER FIVE

STUTTERING

Arthur hated to talk out loud at school. He would stutter so badly he would want to cry, which made the stuttering worse and all the kids would start to laugh.

After recess one day the Sister asked the kids to line up. Arthur stood in front of his brother Norbert. The nun looked at Arthur and he suddenly had a sick feeling in his stomach.

"Arthur," said the Sister. "You haven't said our morning prayer for a long time. I think it shall be your turn." Norbert snickered and poked him in the back.

"Take your turn to say the prayer."

"Not, Not, Notre…" Arthur gulped. Norbert snickered and then a couple of other kids snickered. Arthur's face started to burn. He took a deep breath and closed his eyes, 'If I start to say the word and my mouth wants to repeat a letter then I'll just stop and go slowly and make myself not repeat anything. I know I can do this.'

"Notre," he said and took a breath. "Père___ qui___ est ___ aux ___ cieux."

There was silence in the room. Arthur looked up at the Sister, who was red in the face. Sure, it sounded strange, but he had done it.

He had said the whole sentence without stuttering and he knew that if he tried hard, he could stop stuttering completely. He knew he could do it and never stutter again. He didn't simply smile—he glowed.

❦❖❧

On the weekend the weather plummeted. When the weather was that cold Joe usually left the horses in the barn and made one of the kids walk to the store. For some reason, he decided to go himself and hitched up the sleigh.

"Hey, let's go with Papa," whispered Arthur to his younger sister. "Maybe he'll buy us some candy or something."

"But if we ask him, he'll say no because it's too cold."

"Not if he doesn't know we're with him…" said Arthur.

The pair snuck out of the house and crawled into the back of the sleigh, under a blanket and some hay. Neither of them had their winter coats on, because they didn't want Mama to know they had gone. A little way down the road the two started getting cold, even under the blanket. They started whispering and Joe heard them and stopped the sleigh. They were sent home.

When they got home Berthe already knew they were missing and was really mad. Arthur, between the cold and his stuttering couldn't explain. His mother decided he was the big brother so it was his fault and gave him a licking and sent him upstairs. His younger sister wasn't in trouble; she stayed in the kitchen with Berthe and helped bake a cake

❦❖❧

Arthur believed what he was told. He was told by the nun in grade one that he was the ugliest kid in the class after she had run her fingers through his thick, black curls. Many times, Joe called Arthur names as did some of his siblings. He was called a pig, big head, big cow, useless, stupid and ugly. He never felt comfortable in his own house. He was not wanted by his mother and felt ugly.

His father sometimes, would tease Arthur – more or less to get him mad so that he would stutter. In front of the other kids he would say: "Watch me. I'll get him angry and he will start to stutter." And that is what Joe did until the whole family was laughing because Arthur was now upset and stuttering.

Arthur and his Papa were at the neighbors to do a job for them. They were asked in to eat and Arthur was told to wash his hands. Over the wash stand was a mirror with sides that moved. Arthur could look ahead and also see himself from the sides. He couldn't believe how ugly he was, after seeing himself from all angles. He thought to himself, he didn't want people to see such an ugly guy and be disgusted by him.

When Arthur was a teenager he went to a dance in St. Boniface. The girls were after him. They gave him lots of attention. All Arthur could think was "how come these girls like such ugly guys like me."

❧❖☙

Believe in yourself!

CHAPTER SIX

ALTER BOYS

Arthur had been so careful, after the spelling incident. He knew the Sister was still upset and he didn't want to give her any reason to punish him. It didn't help.

"Arthur," she said to him one morning, "At mass, you touched someone with the plate when they were given the host. You were careless. So, I have decided that a boy like you should not be an altar boy."

Wow—was Arthur ever upset! Altar boys were special. There were only four altar boys: Gilbert Gauthier, Gils Gauthier, Luke Yvon, and Arthur Adam. They helped serve the Priest at mass. Every time Arthur acted as an altar boy; he wore a clean white gown over his dirty torn clothes. It made him feel special, and proud, and clean. He'd listen to the words the priest said and he'd repeat them over and over, learning to say them in Latin. Everything about helping the Priest serve the mass made him feel good about himself. Besides, once a year as a special treat the Priest took them all on a road trip to Winnipeg and dinner at a restaurant and then to explore the Eaton's store. He didn't want to miss that. He was devastated.

The nun saw Arthur's expression and she smiled.

"Papa," Arthur said after supper that night. "The nun says I can't be an altar boy no more."

"What?" said Joe, "She has no right, only the Priest can say that. I will fix her," he said in a quiet voice. That was dangerous. Joe talked quiet like that when he was really mad. For a second Arthur almost felt sorry for the nun.

St. Labre was a small community and the Priest would visit people and sometimes eat lunch or supper with them. A couple of days after the Sister told Arthur he couldn't be an Altar boy the Priest came by the Adam house for a visit.

"So," Joe says to the Priest, "I thought you were the boss of the altar boys."

"Well, I am," says the Father.

"You mean you pick who will be an altar boy? And you will tell someone when they can't be an altar boy no more?"

"Well, yes. That is my decision. Why? Is Arthur unhappy about being an altar boy?"

"Arthur isn't an altar boy. The nun fired him from being an altar boy."

"She can't do that," says the Priest, "only I am the boss of the altar boys."

"Ah," says Joe, "Don't tell me that. She's the boss and she's going to run you by the end of the nose. Maybe you should ask her if you can be the boss because she fired Arthur."

The next school day the Priest went to Arthur's classroom and opened the door.

"Excuse me for interrupting the class," he says to the nun. "I want all the altar boys to come out into the hall for a minute. I want to talk with them."

Arthur and the others stood up and started to go out the door into the hall, but the nun looks at Arthur and points back at his chair.

"Sit down, you." Arthur sat back down.

The Priest realized Arthur wasn't in the hallway with the others. He opens the door of the classroom again and points to Arthur.

"You, Arthur, I'm waiting for you. Come here boy."

"No, I'm punishing him, he's not going to serve Mass." the nun says. "Arthur you sit back down. He can't be an altar boy."

"You have no say in the altar boys," the Priest looks at her. "I am the boss of the altar boys, not you. If I say he's an altar boy than he is. Arthur," he motions, "come here. And you," he says to the nun, "you mind your own business."

When Arthur returned to the classroom the Sister was fuming.

"Arthur," she says in front of all the children. "When you serve the mass and you pass the plate, I don't want you to pass it under me. You touched someone with the plate, and that is not okay."

The next time Arthur was the altar boy at mass, the Sister was there ready to receive the host from the Priest. When the Priest puts it on her tongue, Arthur puts the plate under her chin in case the host falls to the floor. As soon as the Priest goes on to the next person, Arthur looks at the Sister in the eyes and then moves the plate closer to her throat. The Nun backed up and glared. He moved it closer again, and again she backed-up. He couldn't resist—he touched her with the plate and he could see she was really mad. He smiled and moved on to the next person who was receiving the host.

Arthur had a wonderful time on the trip to Winnipeg with the other altar boys. The Priest took six kids in his Volkswagen Bug. They went to the Eaton's store and out for lunch. Arthur rode on an elevator for the first time and they explored all the different floors.

Arthur never thought about the Sister once during that whole trip.

༄༅༄

Don't let others define you.

Arthur at thirteen years old.

CHAPTER SEVEN

MONEY

Arthur was hungry, it never seemed to quit, the ache in the stomach. Saturday was like any other day, except there was no school. The older boys hunted or checked their trap lines and the younger ones played outside after chores, if it wasn't too cold. The kids trapped by snare: rabbit, squirrel, weasel. It was exciting doing that. Rabbit was good for eating as well as the fur was valued. The squirrel and weasels were for the fur and that way the kids could earn some money of their own. Sometimes Arthur had to go with his dad trapping. He liked to see how smart his dad was in the bush and how he could see tracks or the evidence of tracks that were almost invisible. Once Arthur's younger brother, Joseph, was lost in the woods. Joe tracked him along the creek and into the bush and found him. Arthur thought his dad was amazing—but mean. He would tell Arthur so many times that he was going to kill him. He'd get so mad when Arthur or one of the other kids did something wrong that Arthur would pee himself when Joe gave him a licking, and he wasn't the only one. When Arthur went trapping with Joe, and Joe carried a gun, Arthur was terrified he would make a mistake and his dad would shoot him.

Arthur liked to trap with one of his older brothers. He played tricks on him. Once he checked his trap and then his brother's trap. His had a magpie in it, and his brother's trap had a weasel.

"Okay," he said to his brother, "mine is the weasel, and your trap caught a magpie."

"Are you sure?" his brother looked at him.

Arthur was outside. He had finished his chores and didn't want to help his brothers with the traps. His stomach hurt; he was so hungry.

Tip, the dog, ran through the yard with something in his mouth. Curious, Arthur ran after him to see what it was. The dog was lying behind the wood pile and was starting to eat an old crust of bread he had found. Arthur chased the dog away and ate it.

Berthe was shopping today, so they would probably have to eat a piece of bread with lard on it or her homemade margarine with this coloring and oh... did it taste bad, but he'd eat it because there wouldn't be anything else until supper after she got home. Or maybe they would have bread with milk on it, and if Berthe had enough sugar his older sister would let them have a spoonful of sugar on the bread, since Berthe wasn't there. Berthe guarded the sugar. Every two days she made 12 loaves of bread and sometimes they would run out, so she needed the sugar for baking. She bought a hundred pounds of it a month, and two hundred pounds of flour and staples like cornstarch and yeast. The family allowance from the government was $5 a month per child, and that's what paid for the groceries. They had cows for milk and hunted and trapped for meat and extra money. There were chickens for meat and for eggs, and pigs. Berthe only shopped for cornstarch, yeast, flour and sugar and sometimes if she had extra money, she'd buy all the kids chocolate bars.

When Berthe came home from shopping she handed out chocolate to all the children one by one.

"Not for you, Arthur," She said when it was his turn. "You were not a good boy this week."

He watched his brothers and sisters eating the chocolate bars and he tried to think of a way to get one, but Berthe was watching him. She was always watching him. He went outside and sat behind the wood pile to think.

Money—it was money he needed. If he had money, then he'd never be hungry again.

After supper that night, the family all sat around Joe's chair and he told tales about wolves stalking him when he was trapping in the bush. Wonderful stories—terrifying stories—so real Arthur was scared and looked under his chair for a wolf.

Then he saw it—Papa's wallet. He must have cashed in the family allowance cheques or sold some furs when they were in Woodridge because that wallet was bursting with money. Arthur couldn't take his eyes off it. Joe left it sitting on the table, just sitting there. Arthur had to have it. He had to.

Getting up from his chair, he held himself so the others would think he had to pee. Walking past the table he palmed the wallet while everyone else was riveted on Joe's story. Outside he suddenly panicked. He knew Joe would look for it, and if they thought about it, they might realize that he had left the storytelling. Berthe would be watching him to see if he was spending money. She would know he took it.

Arthur ran into the barn and counted the money; $128. It was a fortune! Arthur was really scared. He didn't know how he could keep it and not get caught. For now, he hid the wallet high in the rafters of the barn and then went back into the house quietly and sat down on the floor, so it looked like he'd always been there. He pretended to listen to the story, but he was really thinking of ways to hide the money and spend it only a little bit at a time. If he spent too much, then his Uncle would tell his parents how much he was spending at his store. There were other things in Joe's wallet that he would need like his driver's license and other papers that Arthur couldn't read. Joe was going to be insane with anger. Arthur felt sick to his stomach and was trying to think of how to get out of this and keep all that money.

The next morning Joe was looking for his wallet. He yelled and Berthe yelled and all the kids were looking for the lost wallet. Joe was so angry that all the kids were afraid that he would start hitting them until that wallet was found—for two days they searched.

"If one of you kids stole my wallet," Joe yelled, "I'll find out who it was, and I'll beat him. I didn't bring a thief into this world. I swear I'll kill him."

Arthur was terrified. He believed Joe would kill him. Now he knew he couldn't keep that money, not even one cent.

Arthur went into the barn and put the wallet in his pocket. He had a plan. He went over to the truck and dropped the wallet on the ground a little bit under the vehicle, so it looked like it fell there when Joe got out. Then he ran back into the house to find Norbert.

"Let's go outside to look for the wallet," he said to his brother. "Everyone has looked in the house and, in the barn, let's look in the yard. Nobody has looked there yet."

"Why? Papa said he had it in the house last night. How would it be out there?"

"Well, maybe when Papa did his business it fell out of his pocket. Or when he checked the cows or was unloading the groceries out of the truck. Besides, Papa is so mad that I would rather be outside if he starts hitting."

Trying to get Norbert to see the wallet without making it obvious was not as easy as Arthur thought. He walked over to the truck, and Norbert went into Joe's shed. Arthur went around the side of the truck by the passenger's side and called Norbert over, but he went over to look around the pig pen. Finally, he pretended to find something by the tire and Norbert came running over and almost stepped on the wallet before he saw it.

"Look, Arthur," he yelled, "it's Papa's wallet, I found it." Norbert held it up and then looked at Arthur. "How did you know it was here?"

"I didn't know it was here. I just wanted to get away from Papa before he killed me. You found it. He'll probably be so happy you found it he'll give you some money."

Norbert looked at the wallet and at Arthur again and then ran to the house yelling that he had found Papa's wallet.

Joe was so happy he gave Norbert 25 cents. Everyone was looking at Norbert and at the money Joe had given him, but not Berthe. She was watching Arthur. Arthur looked at her and gulped. She knew.

Arthur learned his lesson. He still needed money, but it wasn't good to take too much because then you'd get caught.

The sisters collected money for the missions. Parents would give the children pennies to bring to school so the Nun could put them in a jar and when there was enough, they would send them in. The kids were told about the poor children in Africa, and how they needed clothes and food and their pennies would help them. The nuns had pictures of them and taught the kids the importance of helping the poor and starving in the world.

Arthur's Mama was a faithful woman and believed in God and the church. She would send her children to school with pennies for the missions whenever she could. But Arthur didn't get it. He was hungry and Berthe gave him pennies for the poor. And when he came to school with money in his pocket—money he earned helping his brothers trap, or doing extra jobs, the Sister would take his money too, not just the pennies his Mama gave him.

Arthur couldn't understand why the little black people in Africa needed his pennies. The more he thought about it the madder he got. He began to hate black people. He saw them in pictures—he never met one. He didn't know anything about them, but he hated them because the Nun took away his pennies to send to them. He ate food out of the garbage at school because he was hungry, and the Sister took away pennies he could spend at the store for something to eat.

Arthur stopped bringing the money to school. He found a tin box and put all the money he earned doing extra jobs in the tin along with any pennies he was given and buried it in the yard where no one would find it. He saved it all.

Sometimes the Sister would ask him where his pennies were because his brothers and sisters would bring pennies to the school. Arthur said he didn't get any, but he watched where the Sister put the little jar of pennies after she collected the ones from the kids. He watched when she left the schoolroom, and when she came back. He watched her like a hawk.

"The nun, she's got the thing," he told Norbert on the way home from school one day. "You know—money for the black people. There's lots of pennies in that jar. It's just sitting there. If the black people don't come and get it, I'm going to go get it."

"You take it and that Nun will give you a lickin'."

"I ain't scared of that Nun."

"If Papa hears about it, then he'll be mad, and he'll give you a lickin too."

Arthur thought about it. He had to figure out a way to get the pennies and not get caught.

The next day at school Arthur and Norbert waited until the classroom was empty. Norbert stayed at the door and watched in case someone came up the stairs while Arthur took the jar and emptied the pennies into his pocket. The two then went to the corner of the playground to count the money and hide it until after school. It was 22 cents. The two split the money and then talked about how to spend it so the Nun wouldn't know it was them. Arthur hid his with the rest of his money.

The nun knew the money was gone the next day. The first one she asked was Arthur.

"I want to talk to you," she says. She was very upset and saddened. It was serious things to her, to have someone steal money set aside for the poor. "Somebody has stolen the bank. Did you take it?"

"Everything that goes wrong in your life," Arthur says to her, "and somehow it's always my fault."

"So, maybe it wasn't you. Do you know who it was?"

"Yes, I think I know who it is," Arthur says. 'Okay,' he thinks to himself 'who is the meanest person I know so she might be too afraid to ask him about the money.'

"Who was it?" Asked the Nun.

"My brother, David," Arthur smiled to himself. He loved his brother David, but David was mean and tough. He was a fighter, and he didn't put up with anything, not even from Joe. The Nun would never cross David, she'd be too afraid.

"Go downstairs and get David," the nun told him.

Arthur looked at her, stunned. He got up and left the classroom and started going down the stairs slowly. He was feeling bad. He didn't want David to get into trouble; he really didn't think the Nun would confront him because of his reputation. And now she's going to ask him if he did it and he'll say no. If David gets into trouble, then he will tell everyone he didn't do it and Norbert knew it was Arthur who stole it.

Arthur knocked on the door of the downstairs classroom and said to the nun, "Sister, the sister upstairs wants David to go up to talk to her."

His brother was already in a bad mood. He was checking his traps before school and had arrived late. The Nun had given him a licking with a ruler across his knuckles.

David goes up the stairs stomping. Then he grabs the door and it flies open, banging against the wall.

"What do you want?" he says to the nun.

"You stole the bank?"

"Tu mens," which in English means "You lie."

The nun didn't know what to do with that. She didn't want to deal with him and sent him back downstairs.

A few years later when Arthur went to Winnipeg to find work, he saw a black man on the street. 'This is the guy who's got my money.' He thought to himself as he walked up to the man.

"Did you get it?" Asked Arthur.

"What?" Said the black man.

"I been sending money to little black people in Africa since I was a kid."

"What are you talking about?"

"Aren't you from Africa?" said Arthur.

"No, I'm from Jamaica and I never got a dime," The man was getting angry. "I used to send money to little white people in Canada," He said, "Did you ever get any?"

≈❖≈

A bad experience is your best teacher!

PART TWO

THE TRAIL

Son, I'm sure he thought we were nuts -- the trucker we stopped on the way to the bush camp. Nobody in Manitoba drives in on a Sunday night in wintertime. They're too smart. They go in the morning when there is traffic in case you get stuck. But I can't wait for nothing.

The trucker tells us the camp is four miles in, then he leaves and we keep driving. We're driving this little four-banger and the snow keeps getting under the hood and is getting everything wet under there. Somehow, the electrical, it all shorts out and the car dies. It's died for no good reason. No heat, no lights, no nothing.

That piece of garbage.

Now we're sitting in this little car in the middle of the bush at 10:30 at night and we know the chance of anybody else coming down that road before morning is really slim. Of course, the best thing we could do was stay in the car. The worst thing I could ever do was leave that car. I know that because it is Sunday night and everybody goes in to camp Monday morning—except for two French nuts—me and Leo. And me? I gotta prove everything—Okay, I'm thinking I'd be a coward if I stay in that car. I'm the big brother here. I have to save the day.

"Leo," I tell your uncle, "I'm walking in to the camp from here. That trucker, he said it was four miles. I can do that easy."

"You stay here," he says to me. "It's got to be 38 below or even colder out there. Two of us in the car out of the wind, we'll stay warmer."

"I'm not staying here. I'm walking in. Look Leo," I say. "Only one track in the snow belonging to that trucker—no other tracks—nothing. Nobody will come and we'll freeze. If I'm wrong and someone does come, then you and him pick me up."

I pull on my second pair of jeans over the pair I'm already wearing. I got no mitts. I just got gloves with the fingers and boots and a toque—no ear flaps—no parka. A parka is useless when you work in the bush. You can't move your arms cutting and stripping trees. I just got a work jacket with a sweater under it.

"There will be trucks and gas at the camp." I tell him. "When I get there, I'll light the stove and then drive back to get you. You'll see."

I walk off alone down this road with bush on both sides. The moon on the snow makes it bright. My breath is hot coming from my mouth and nose and I can feel the moisture building ice on my face. I wonder if I'm making a mistake. When I take a breath, the freezing air makes my lungs hurt. I wish I had a scarf or better yet a toque that goes down over the face with holes for the eyes and mouth.

I don't.

Okay, now it's getting hard to walk. I stop and bend over with my hands between my legs to get some warmth. My fingers ache. It's hard to breathe and I think of being held under the covers when I was little. I'd feel the heat rise to my face and the panic with my heart beating up into my throat. I'd hear my older brother laugh as I flailed helplessly, in the dark, struggling to breathe.

I stay like that for a few minutes—I'm home, I'm little again…

When you walk in heavy snow, Son, it feels like you're sliding back steady. I started to have doubts—about the mistake I made. I started to have doubts about what I decided to do when I was no more than a half mile away. I started thinking, you know what? Should I turn around? And don't ask me why I kept going, Son. And lots of times, I'm thinking, should I turn around? Should I turn around? Somehow, I did not turn around, I'm just that kind of person—I just gotta keep going.

In five minutes, maybe, the two pairs of jeans are cold and stiff. With every step I feel them grinding off skin; and no warmth, them. I could be wearing cardboard. But okay, I'm stubborn. I don't look back at that little car. I keep walking; boots sliding on the frozen chunks of snow; a light breeze throwing ice crystals at my bare skin. But Son, it is only four miles.

As a kid I was always afraid of the bush; of what the bush hides; what is in there. In the dark mornings when I did the chores before breakfast, I could feel the eyes watching me; eyes of wolves or bears. Okay, I have always been afraid of the bears, Son. Always afraid I will meet a bear and me, without a gun. For years I round up the cows in the bush and worry about animals that want to eat me—okay, I'm scared.

"You are too little for a gun," Your Grandpa said to me. "You have to be big enough to hold it up first, eh?"

But I guess I was not so little to go out into the bush alone to find the cows and face a bear or a wolf maybe. Sure, I was scared. The fear, it made me work hard to get big—big so I could have a gun before the animals ate me.

I don't have a gun with me tonight. I look at the black shadows under the trees. Maybe the thoughts of wild animals are not such a good idea right now. Bears are sleeping, but wolves aren't.

The moon is shining down. The snow glows white on the ground, making the shadows of the trees black—did that shadow move? I stop and stare at it. I think I hear a snap behind me. I look back on the trail. No car in sight. I think I must have walked a mile—too far for the car to help me. I can't out-run a wolf. My heart is pounding in my ears. I listen hard to the night and squint, trying to see through the trees; to see if I can see glowing eyes...

CHAPTER EIGHT

THE FINGER

Arthur's older brother Pierre helped Joe in the bush. He got a cut on his finger, but it wasn't bad. It was just a little cut, not deep even and Pierre didn't think anything of it. He and Joe worked for the municipality fixing the roads. Most of the job was picking stones. The municipality brought in trucks first and sprayed poison along the road to kill the trees and weeds. A few days later, Joe and Pierre started work clearing away the stones. Somehow, some of the poison found its way into Pierre's cut on his finger. He felt the stinging, but again, he didn't think anything of it. By the end of the day his finger was throbbing and swollen. The next day it was so big and sore he couldn't bend it and he wouldn't let anyone touch it and he couldn't work—which made Joe really angry.

"Joseph," Berthe said to Joe the next morning, "Pierre has to go to the doctor with that finger."

"Ah! Tabarnak! I'm not taking a day off work to take him to the doctor with a little cut. He's missing work already. We'll see how it is tomorrow."

By evening the finger was bigger and looked bruised and the infection seeped.

"Joseph, he needs to go to the doctor. Uncle is going to the Chiropractor tomorrow in Steinbach; he said he'd take Pierre in with him."

"All this for a little finger? Mon Dieu!"

Pierre went in with his uncle and the Chiropractor told Pierre he needed to go to the hospital right away because it looked like there was blood poisoning. Without getting permission from Joe, the uncle took Pierre to the hospital in Winnipeg where they operated right away. There were lines from the cut all the way to his elbow. He almost died, but they operated in time and Pierre kept his arm. He was in hospital for a few days.

All the boys helped with wood and got slivers all the time, but after what happened to Pierre everyone paid more attention, especially Arthur. It scared him to think that a little cut or sliver could cause blood poisoning and kill someone. Every night before bed, he checked his hands for slivers and one night, his worst fear came true. He found a sliver so deep in his finger, he couldn't get it out. By morning it was sore—probably from all the squeezing and poking.

By the end of the day it was swollen and looked infected. The next morning, he couldn't milk because the finger was too sore to bend. Berthe looked at it and laughed.

"Arthur," she said to him before school, "it's just a simple sliver. Leave it alone and it will pop out on its own."

Arthur didn't believe it. All the way to school, he worried that his finger was getting blood poisoning like Pierre's. At recess, he showed the Sister at school and she seemed really concerned.

"You need to go home," she said to him. "Tell your dad to take you to the doctor and get that seen to. You tell him that I am telling him he has to take a day off work and drive you to the doctor. If you get blood poisoning in your vein, you could die in a couple of hours. You tell him you need to go right away and have it looked at because it could go really bad as quick as a couple of hours. You tell your dad I said that—tell him I said he has to take you now."

Arthur ran out of the school and down those steps as fast as he could. He was terrified. He didn't want to die. He ran in a blind panic down the road, holding his finger close to his chest.

"Oh, God," He prayed, "let me get home and get to the doctor before that poison kills me. Help me get to the doctor before two hours so I don't die. Please God, make Papa listen and take me right away, I don't want to die."

'Oh, no!' he thought. 'What if Papa wasn't home? What if he was in Woodridge and there was no one at the neighbors who could take me before I died in two hours? How will my family find me after I died?'

The more he thought the more he was afraid and worried. If Papa wasn't home by the time he did get there, it would be too late to save him.

"Please God," he prayed out loud, 'Let Papa be home.' In his head, he saw the coffin they would be buying in a week. He did not want to die. He was afraid that they would bury him in the cemetery by the church, and he didn't want to be buried there. He ran faster, holding his finger, running down the middle of the road.

'What if the nun is wrong?' he thought. 'What if I don't have two hours? What if I only have one hour?'

Arthur stopped running and stood in the road. He didn't know what to do. He knew he had to run two kilometers down the road before he would turn onto the road where they lived. After that he'd have to run another kilometer to his house. If he took the short cut through the field and the bush to go home, he'd save about six minutes.

'Maybe the nun is wrong,' he thought. 'Maybe I won't make it home at all. What if I die along the way? Should I take the short cut through the bush? It is shorter and I'll get there sooner, but what if it is still too late? If I take the short cut and die in the bush, then no one will find me. My body will stay there and Mama will never know what happened to me. I won't be buried in the cemetery or have a mass said and pennies paid to the Priest to get my soul out of purgatory. If I stay on the road, which is longer, and if I die, I know someone will at least find my body so it doesn't get eaten by wolves and wild animals.'

"But I don't want to die at all," he said out loud, choking back the fear. "I'll take the short cut and run so hard that if I drop dead my body will skid another fifteen meters before it stops, so then at least they will find me."

With sweat filling his arm pits, breath ragged and heart throbbing in his throat, he ran flat out as fast as he could.

As Arthur burst into from the bush and into the clearing around his house, he could hear the boys cutting wood.

'Good, Papa is home,' he thought. 'He can take me to the hospital.'

"Papa," he yelled breathlessly, "Papa, I have to go to the doctor. The nun said I only had two hours before I was going to die and it took me twenty minutes to run home and so I only have an hour and forty minutes left for you to drive me to the doctor and save my life. Look at my finger." He thrust it into Joe's face. "The Sister said, Papa. She told me to tell you that she says you HAVE to take me to the hospital right now or it will be too late. She said she's TELLING you to take me right now."

"Hmmm," said Joe as he inspects the dirty finger. "So, the nun is telling me to take you. She said this is going to kill you?"

"Yes Papa, in just two hours."

"She said you would die from this in two hours?"

"Yes, and now I only have an hour and a half left. She said the poison is traveling up my arm and I'm going to die. Papa, I only got maybe an hour before I die. You got to drive me to the hospital."

"An hour?"

"Yes, Papa, I only got an hour before I die—the Sister said."

"Well, if you got an hour before you die, here's the axe, you got time to split some wood," said Joe.

Don't leave for tomorrow, what you can do today!

CHAPTER NINE

THE COOKIES

Arthur's great-uncle owns the store, which is just a room in the front of his house. Everyone says he's the richest man in St. Labre, because everybody has to buy from him. Only a few people use cash. Most people sell things to the store for credit, and then buy on account based on the amount of their credit. The Adams sell furs, or eggs, or milk, or firewood, chickens… anything the store will take. No money changes hands. The Uncle takes the furs and wares to Woodridge to sell so he's the only one who gets money. Besides what the Adam's farm supplies to the store, Joe works on the roads for the municipality, or clears land for cash. The Adam family also receive a family allowance cheque from the government every month. The government pays them $5.94 per child under the age of sixteen. The girls can live at home until they get married but the boys have to leave when the government money stops or when they are too big for Joe to control.

The Uncle always looked mad to Arthur. He talked rough and he was kind of mean. The kids laughed at him. He was married to Arthur's Grandma's sister. He was from France originally and a very hard worker. He went to church all the time.

Joe often sent the kids to go and pick things up from the store. For a while the family had no money at all and charged food on an account at the store.

Well, on the way home from school one day Arthur figured out that since Joe always sent them to the store and his Uncle was used to the kids charging on account, he would go and get a package of Maple Leaf cookies. There were five rows of cookies in a box and they were five walking together on the way home. They were so hungry and they still had chores before supper. They all agreed not to tell and each of them got a row of cookies. They did it every day until Joe found out and he was mad. The kids ran and he threw wood at them and waved his belt above his head before bringing it down on a struggling kid. He kicked them, and hit them wherever on their bodies he could catch.

He screamed at them and Arthur was terrified. He found a place under the corner of the wood pile and stayed there until Joe had spent all his anger.

At Christmas time the church was all decorated inside and smelled of evergreen and incense. The school put on a pageant and the kids got candy and a dollar each from the school. At home, Arthur's family would have a tree, but nothing under it. Berthe made a special meal for Christmas and they would all walk to the church for midnight mass. Then Joe would take away their dollars. One of the older boys argued and refused to give up his dollar. Joe grabbed him and started to hit him, yelling and cursing. He kept hitting, and hitting. Then he took the boy outside and told him to stay there.

Joe got his dollar.

Merry Christmas!

❧❖☙

Rise above your upbringing and things that made you suffer.

CHAPTER TEN

THE PEANUT

Arthur saw Joe's coat lying on a chair. Joe was listening to the radio and smoking. Supper was over and everyone had finished their chores. Arthur was still hungry, and he knew Berthe would not give him more to eat. He couldn't go to the store and charge anything on the account—not after what happened the last time. He knew if he was going to get anything to eat, he'd have to sneak it, or get some money to buy something.

Arthur looked over at Joe. He wasn't paying attention to what Arthur was doing so he thought he might check Joe's coat pockets in case there was money he could take. It was lying on a chair. Arthur, keeping his eyes on Joe walked over to the coat. Joe wasn't even looking at him. Keeping his eyes on Joe he reached into a pocket and found fifty cents.

Smiling, he put the money in his pocket and went outside. It was still light outside, even though it was getting late. If he hurried, he could get to the store before his Uncle locked the door. But he didn't want to go alone in case it was dark before he got home.

"Norbert," he called to his brother. "I got some money and I want to go to the store and buy some peanuts. Come with me and we'll split them."

"No, you won't. You want me to come because it's almost dark, but as soon as you get the peanuts you'll go and hide and eat them all yourself."

"No, Norbert I won't. Just come with me, I promise."

"I'll come but if you don't give me half then I'm going to tell Papa you stole money," he said.

They take off down the road and half way to the store it started to get really dark. Their Uncle had closed the store and locked the door. Arthur banged on the door and yelled.

"What the heck do you want? The store is closed," his Uncle sounded really mad.

"Uncle, it's Arthur. Papa sent me for some peanuts." He knocked again hard and yelled. "He'll be so mad at me if I don't bring them for him." Uncle opened the door and looked out.

"Joe sent you boys here for peanuts? It's so late."

"Yes, Papa sent us. He gave us fifty cents to buy him peanuts, see." Arthur held out the coins.

Uncle let them in. Fifty cents in those days bought an enormous bag of peanuts—the kind with the shells on. Arthur took hold of that bag and he could hardly wait to find a place to eat the peanuts. His mouth was watering.

"When we get home, Norbert," he said to his brother, "we can't let the others see the peanuts or they will tell. I'll go and take them to the barn and hide them and we can split them later."

"No, Art. You're trying to trick me. I want my half peanuts right now. If you don't give them to me right now, then I'm telling Papa you stole money from him and bought peanuts."

Arthur didn't want another beating from Joe, and would have given Norbert the whole bag to keep him quiet if he had to. They didn't want the Uncle to look out and see them dividing the peanuts, because they were supposed to be for Joe. The boys went over to the church to find a place to hide while they divided them, but there was a meeting starting and too many people.

"Let's go to the cemetery," said Norbert. "We can hide behind a headstone while you give me my half."

The gate was locked, but there was enough room for the boys to crawl underneath. As Arthur wiggled under the corner of the peanut bag got caught on the gate and ripped. In the moon light they saw three peanuts fall out, but could only find two of them.

Finding a head stone big enough to hide them, they sat down, opened the bag and started counting.

"This one's for you," said Arthur, "and here, you can take this one and this one's for me, and here's one for you."

"I want this one," said Norbert, "and these two and here are three for you."

"Okay, so this one is yours and this one is mine."

At this time a deacon of the church was hurrying to get to the meeting at the church, as he was late. He decided to take a short cut in front of the cemetery just as the boys were dividing the peanuts. It was really dark by then. The deacon heard the boys two voices and looked around to see who it was but couldn't see anyone. All he could see was headstones.

"One for me, one for you," said Arthur

"One for me, one for you."

"Here is the last one," Said Arthur. "I'll take this one."

"No," said Norbert. "This one is mine."

"You can have the one at the gate."

The man at the gate ran to the Church and into the meeting.

"Everybody," He says, "we need to pray really hard. Folks, let's get right with God. On my way here I passed in front of the cemetery and I heard God and the devil arguing over our souls. They were dividing us up between them. And one of them just about got me."

The news went through the community like wildfire. Norbert and Arthur knew the truth, but they just ate their peanuts and didn't say a word.

Knowledge is power!

CHAPTER ELEVEN

THE WATCH

"Arthur," said Berthe, "you know you haven't been going to confession for a long time. You better go to confession when you go to communion, I'll be watching you. To make sure you go."

'Ah, me,' thought Arthur.

"Norbert, you come with me to church for communion. Mama says you have to go to confession because you are such a bad boy."

"Ha," said Norbert, "she told me to go with you to church to make sure you go to confession, so now I think I will watch you."

The confession booth has three sections connected by a little window with a door. The Priest sits in the middle and people go in and sit on either side, taking turns. Confession is before communion, so there are usually lots of people and they wait in line until it's their turn.

Arthur shoved Norbert into the line ahead of him, and he was the last one waiting for confession. He didn't think he had done anything wrong, so he needed time to think of something to tell the Priest.

What am I going to tell him? I always say to him, I say Father, I have sinned, I said a lie or I said bad words. I don't know what to say, I have no sin.

What am I going to tell this guy—the Priest— when I get in there?' thought Arthur.

"What are you going to say, Norbert?"

"That's private, Arthur."

"But you can tell me, I won't tell."

"Not going to."

"How come?"

"What are you going to say?"

"I don't know."

"You better say something or Mama will know."

Finally, Norbert and Arthur are the only ones left in line. Norbert goes into his section and he was in there a long time. Arthur was starting to worry. He didn't know what he was going to say, and then he saw the Priest's coat on the hook on the outside of the confessional. There was no one else in the church, and so Arthur walked up to the coat and reached into the pocket. He felt something cold and pulled it out. It was the Priest's pocket watch.

Arthur smiled. *'Now I have something to confess,'* he thought to himself.

The last person left the cubicle and Arthur went in and shut the door and knelt down, waiting until the Priest was finished with Norbert on the other side. Then the Priest opens the little door between the cubicles.

"May the Lord be in your heart to help you make a good confession," said the Priest.

"Bless me, Father, for I have sinned. It has been a long time since my last Confession. Father, I have sinned against you and against the Highest."

He said, "What did you do?"

Arthur says, "I stole a watch."

"Well," said the Priest, "You've got to give it back to the one you stole it from."

"Here," Arthur says and holds it out to him. It was dark in the confessional and the Priest couldn't see what the boy was holding.

"I don't want it," he said to Arthur. "Give it back to the one you stole it from, that's your penance."

"Well," said Arthur. "I tried to give it back to him, but he didn't want it."

"Okay," he said, "keep it then, it's not stolen. Have you anything else to confess, my son."

"No, Father."

"Your sins are forgiven; go in peace."

"Thanks be to God, and to you, Father," says Arthur.

After the priest got out of the confessional, he noticed that his watch no longer was in his jacket pocket and realized that Arthur was the one who had stolen it. After Mass, he went to talk to Arthur but Arthur started running and the priest ran behind him to try and catch him, with a twig in his hand.

When we were young, it was believed that once you confess your sins, the priest forgets all he's heard in the confessional. He obviously did not forget Arthur's sins. Arthur gave him back his watch eventually.

❧✣☙

If you make a mistake, apologize and move on.

The old farmyard when Arthur was growing up.

The old farmyard as it looks today.

CHAPTER TWELVE

THE TRUCK

As Arthur got older his hunger got worse. It occupied his mind all the time. At eleven years old he was still in grade two. He couldn't read or write, and the Sisters didn't know what to do with him, so he stayed where he was.

One day he made this deal with his two cousins.

"You give me one sandwich a day for a year, and I'll build you a truck." He told them. "I know how to build a truck, and I'll build you a truck." Of course, he didn't know how to build a truck and didn't know how to convince them to keep giving him food before they figured it out, but he decided he'd worry about that later.

"If you want this truck then you can't tell your mom and dad or the nuns or anyone that I'm building you a truck and you are paying me in sandwiches." It had to be secret, so no one could catch him with the sandwiches. If one of his brothers or sisters or a nun catches him with a sandwich then his cousins will find out that the truck is a lie and he'd lose the sandwiches.

His cousins agreed. Every day at school they brought an extra sandwich in their lunches for him. He would eat the two slices of bread from home and then bite into real sandwiches afterwards. He was in heaven.

"When can we see our truck?" They asked him after about a month or two. "Is it at your house? Can we come over on Saturday to see it?"

"Oh, not yet. But soon, when I need some help lifting the engine in, then you can come and help. But not yet 'cause I don't want my brothers to know 'cause they'd get jealous."

Arthur worried about losing his sandwiches at school. He had to keep them happy so they'd keep bringing them to him for a whole year. He thought maybe build a wagon maybe, and pretend to put a motor on it—anything. Every day at lunchtime they wanted to hear his progress. He made stuff up and kept them excited. Privately he was thinking, *I'll build this wagon, I'll take this piece of wood and put a cover of a jam lid on it for the steering wheel and if I find four peanut butter or jam cans for the wheels—but then we only buy one can a year so it would take four years to build this truck and they won't wait that long.*

After another month, Arthur finds this old washing machine with a ringer on it.

'I'm going to make them believe that this is the truck I'm making for them,' he thinks to himself. He digs through the scrap heap at home and finds some rims and makes little wheels. He builds a crossbar on the washing machine to sit on.

Finally, they've had enough of waiting and they demanded to see the truck.

"Yeah, well I'm having a problem with it," he told them. "It doesn't want to start. So, I'm going to bring it as soon as I can get it to start."

After a while they demanded again that they see this truck. They brought him a sandwich but they wouldn't give it to him until they saw the truck.

"I brought it to school," he told them. "I hid it in the bush so no one can find it." They wanted to see it, but of course there wasn't a truck and so he couldn't show it to them. They were so mad they told the nun that Arthur had a truck he made and had hid it in the bushes.

"Go get that truck and bring it here," she said.

"I don't have a truck," he said.

"I had to tell her that," he told his cousins. "Otherwise, she'd tell my parents and my dad would take it away and then you would never get your truck. I'll bring it to school on Friday."

On Friday, Arthur brought the wringer washer with wheels and jam lids to school and hid it in the bushes. The cousins followed him out of the school after eating lunch, and they were so excited to finally see their truck. They weren't happy because it wouldn't start and didn't really look like a real truck, but they took it home anyway.

"That's not a truck, it's a wringer washing machine," said their father when he stopped laughing.

Arthur was relieved—until Church that Sunday when his Uncle told his parents what he had done and Joe brought up the truck at the supper table.

"What is this? This truck you are building for your cousins?"

Arthur stumbled over his words, trying to avoid the mention of the food. Joe exploded and swung his arm to cuff him while he cursed. Arthur ducked his head and Joe's hand hit the plate of food on the table. It flew all over the place. Joe grabbed Arthur and he ended up with his hands and hair filled with food.

"Tabarnak!" He screamed, "Why would you do something like that? And now here I am, I just came home from church and already you are making me swear!"

∾❖๛

Don't be scared to to take chances and make mistakes.

Arthur at sixteen years of age.

CHAPTER THIRTEEN

FOOD

Berthe watched Arthur closely, and Arthur knew it. He knew his Mama loved him, but he knew she didn't like him very much. So, he figured he had to be sneaky.

Arthur never missed an opportunity to eat. If there wasn't an opportunity, then he made one. He was always hungry.

Arthur knew there were Saskatoon bushes loaded with berries. He got a can, went out and filled it up with berries and some sugar, then put it on the stove to get hot. He waited until it was nice and hot and then sat down at the table and ate it.

'Okay, that was good,' he thought to himself.

He looked at Berthe. She had her back to him. He went and got some more berries and put them in his can, but when he tried to get some sugar to put on them Berthe stopped him.

"No more sugar. You have berries; that's enough."

He put the can on the stove and he's waiting for his Mama to turn around, but she kept watching him.

When the berries were hot, Arthur sat down and ate them. They weren't that good, they were sour.

'Hm,' he thought. *'She watches me when I came back with berries, but not before.'*

Arthur went over to the sugar and put some in the bottom of his can. His Mama didn't turn around. Then he went outside to pick more berries and she started watching him again to make sure he didn't go for the sugar. She didn't know he already had the sugar in the can under the berries.

Thinking he was really smart, he put the can on the stove and because the sugar was on the bottom it started to sizzle and foam and she knew by the smell what he had done.

That was the end of his berries.

❧ ❖ ☙

There was a piece of bread on the table after breakfast and he noticed that in the pot there was porridge. Arthur knew that Berthe was still angry about the extra toast so he knew she would never let him have the bread. Arthur knew full well that his mother wouldn't give it to him.

He decided to get Norbert to ask for the bread. If he asked, she would give it to him. But he had to come up with a way to get Norbert to give it to him.

"Norbert," he said, "I'll make you a deal." They were outside in the barn, "go in the house, there's a piece of bread on the table, soak it into the porridge and you give it to me. I have 5 cents, and I'll give it to you." Well, he didn't want to give him his 5 cents, but figured Norbert would do what he wanted and when he brought him the bread Arthur would tell him he changed his mind and didn't want it. Norbert wouldn't eat the porridge, so he'd give it to Arthur anyway and Arthur would keep his money.

Norbert said, "Okay" and went into the house.

"I'm hungry, Mama," he said, "Can I have this piece of bread?"

"Yes, you can," she said. Norbert took the bread and put it in the porridge to soak it. Berthe watched him and figured out something was up.

"What are you doing? You going to eat that?"

"No, I'm not."

"Well," she said, "What are you going to do with it?"

"Arthur said that if I got the bread and soaked it in the porridge then he'd give me 5 cents for it."

"Okay, Bert," she said. "You go and give that to him and tell him I said he has to give you the 5 cents."

❧✥☙

The family dog's name was Tip, and there were cats, lots of them. The animals stayed outside, except sometimes if there was a mouse, a cat was brought in to clear up the problem.

Arthur loved to sit close to his dad's chair when they had friends over, and listen to the grownups talk. If he was really quiet, no one noticed. Although most of the time he was permitted to sit there because he needed to do homework—which he hated—so Mama let him stay downstairs so she could make sure he was working on it.

One evening there were a few of his parent's friends over. Arthur was sitting on the floor next his dad's chair and was supposed to be working on his spelling—which was open on the floor in front of him.

Arthur was petting the cat.

He had an idea. He had a plastic ball, some string, and scotch tape. The cat kept trying to play with the ball, which was where Arthur got the idea. He taped the string to the cat's tail while he kept the cat distracted by petting him. On the other end of the string he taped the ball to the tail.

Everything was set. Arthur packed up his spelling, and quietly slipped away to watch. The cat soon realized the ball was attached to his tail and he started to go crazy, running at least five times around the room on the floor, jumping on things to get away from the ball that was taped to his tail. And Joe said, "What the heck got into that cat?"

If you are sure about everything, you are a loser.

CHAPTER FOURTEEN

CHURCH

When Arthur's family went to midnight mass, they all walked. Arthur like going to church in the evening, but he was scared to walk in the dark. Every Sunday they went to church to take communion at 10 o'clock in the morning. They would all pile into the truck, with Berthe, Joe and the littlest ones in the front cab and the rest in the box standing up like sardines because there wasn't room to sit down.

None of them wore hats on their heads, just little coats. They were tough like nails.

No one was allowed to eat before communion, which was agonizing for Arthur. By the time church was over he was famished. Communion was served at 8:30 a.m. at the church too, but Berthe didn't make a meal until after Church was over so there was no advantage in going earlier.

Until Arthur figured out a way of getting around it.

"Mama," he said. "I'm going to take communion earlier today, okay?"

Berthe looked at him. She was sure he was up to something but for the life of her she couldn't figure out what.

"You will have to walk, and you can't have anything to eat until I come home and make lunch."

I know.

Off he went with a big smile on his face as Berthe watched him out the window. He walked along the road slowly until he got to the creek and he decided to go poke around in the water for a bit. Taking his time, he arrived at his Uncle's house close to 9:30, and knocked on the door.

"What can I do for you," said his Uncle.

"I went to communion and I'm so hungry, I can't wait until my Mom makes us dinner," said Arthur. "Could I have a cracker or a cookie or something so I can wait until everyone else comes home for lunch?"

"Oh, okay," says his Uncle. When he's sitting at the table his Uncle brings him a huge piece of pie. Arthur was in heaven and couldn't believe he hadn't thought of this before. He ate the pie so fast his Aunt gave him a second piece with a big glass of milk.

Thanking his Aunt and Uncle he slowly walked home to wait for lunch.

This is too good to quit,' he thought. So, he did it again the next week. When he turned up again the third Sunday in a row, his aunt and uncle started to catch on. At church they asked one of the altar boys if Arthur had been to communion earlier and of course he said no.

"Oh," said his aunt. "I wondered because he's been coming to our house to eat before coming to church." Arthur's little sister was standing next to her aunt and overheard the comment.

Berthe was furious when she found out.

.

❧❖☙

Joe always said school was stupid. He also hated the nuns and complained about the Priests.

There were many Priests in St. Labre who came and went over the years. It was a Roman Catholic town, being named after Saint

Benoit Joseph Labre from Quebec.

The Priest in the town of St. Labre was Father Giroux. Joe really liked him, although he took every opportunity to give him a bad time, always jokingly of course.

Father Giroux was skinny with blonde hair he kept in a brush-cut. He had a long nose and kind blue eyes. The boys liked him because he was a real guy. He liked women, and there were lots of rumors around but there are always rumors in a small town.

Father Giroux ate at the Adam's house often. If he saw the kids walking to school, he gives them a lift or when he was going to their house for dinner, he'd give them all a ride home from the school. And he joked with the boys about women.

"You talk about temptation but you know, I can go out with a woman and trust myself with her—you know—and not go too far," one of Arthur's brothers said one time.

"I am a Priest," smiled Father Giroux, "I wouldn't even trust myself." It must have been true since years later he left the Priesthood and got married.

The Adam family had invited him for lunch one Sunday; he declined, saying he wasn't feeling well. Later Joe saw him in Vassar ice-skating with some women.

"I thought you were sick," Joe said to Father Giroux at church the next Sunday.

"Yeah," says Giroux, "I was."

"Don't lie to me. Last week you told me you're sick and then later I saw you in Vassar and you were with young women. Let me ask you a question. What is the difference between Jesus Christ and you? Jesus Christ draws his sheep to him; you don't care for the sheep; you send the dog after them."

But no matter how much he complained about the Priests and the nuns, he always made sure the family went to church.

The Catholic Church in St. Labre was small and made of wood. There was only plain glass in the windows and no carpets just wood floors. It was so quiet during the service you could hear a mouse a mile away, especially when they prayed and the Lord came down and inhabited the host for communion.

One morning Arthur's family was sitting in the pews they always sat in. Joe didn't have to say anything if someone was doing something wrong, he just had to give them "the look" and that's all it took.

Arthur was sitting next to one of his sisters and right at the time when everyone is praying and there's no noise in the church at all, the two started to giggle. Joe gave them "the look". Arthur's sister saw the look and nudged Arthur. One look at his dad and he stopped giggling. Joe gave him an "You will get it when you get home" look and Arthur looks down at his feet.

As soon as they get home Joe starts to bitch, and when he starts, he carries on, and on. "You two," he says to his brothers, "you two. You arrive to church late. What are you doing even going to church? You don't deserve to be there, why do you even go?"

"And you, he says to another brother who was an altar boy, you stand up there in front of everyone in town and you—you can't stand with your legs together? You are all crooked and can't stand straight?"

"And you last week?" He swings around and shakes his finger at Arthur. "Don't you know how to be an altar boy?"

❧ ❖ ☙

You are not the person you were when you were young. You change.

CHAPTER FIFTEEN

THE BEATING

When Arthur's parents went shopping or to dances or just out for the evening, the older siblings looked after the younger ones. One of Arthur's older brothers was mean to the younger ones and even beat them up if they didn't do what he wanted. He'd line up all the little kids at the bottom of the stairs and tell them to run up them as fast as they could for a race, and then he would run right over them all. The little kids were stepped on and they fell on the steps or knocked against the posts as he trampled them. At night he used to hold Arthur under the covers and do things that made Arthur angry and disgusted. He was a bully, and loved to hold him under there and not let him out until Arthur was fighting and crying. As he grew up, claustrophobia haunted him and he battled it for years.

Arthur also had a sister who looked after the little ones sometimes, when their parents were out. She had a punishment for Arthur, if he was bad. She would make him play with her, make him lay on top of her and she would drag him up and down, or he would have to rub her with his fingers, which she called scratching. She was thirteen at the time and Arthur only six when it started. He didn't know why she wanted him to do it, and he didn't tell Berthe because his sister only made him do it if he was bad and it was better than getting a licking.

"Arthur," she'd say to him. If you don't listen to me, you'll have to come upstairs and scratch."

Arthur thought she was the devil.

About a year after it started the family was sitting around the dinner table and talking. Often this was when Joe would tell stories, but not this time. Arthur was angry. He had been in trouble since the minute he got up. He had a tough day at school and one of his brothers was picking on him and he was simply miserable. One of his brothers told his parents about something Arthur had done and the others were teasing him, saying he was going to get a licking. Arthur had had enough. He exploded.

"Okay—it's not my fault," he yelled. "I do my best and nobody sees it; I still get in trouble, me. And the rest of you, Mama brings you chocolate bars and I get none because she says I'm bad. And you," he points to one of his brothers, "you make us run up the stairs and then you step on us. And at night you hold me under the covers and do things to me, and you," He points to his sister, "You make me lay on you and scratch you. But I'm always the one who gets in trouble and I'm sick of it."

The conversation carried on and Joe started telling a story as if Arthur hadn't said a word. Arthur's brother and his sister were both staying quiet and looking down at the table. Berthe wasn't talking either, she looked at Arthur's brother and he squirmed, but looked right back at her. She then looked at his sister and she looked at her Mama as if she was going to cry. Then Berthe looked at Arthur and he was still mad and stared back at her defiantly.

After dinner was put away and the kids were cleaning up, Berthe and Arthur's older sister went outside for a talk. Arthur went to bed and his brother was mad, but left him alone.

When Arthur got home from school the next day, Berthe took him outside to the barn. She yelled at him and called him a dirty boy. She kept yelling that he should never, never do those things again.

She grabbed a stick of firewood and started to hit him as she yelled. She hung on to his arm so he couldn't run and as he cried and yelled and twisted to get away, he was hit on his bum, and legs, and arms and on his wrists and head—whatever was in reach. It was like she hit with hate. Arthur finally broke away and ran into the bush crying. He kept running until he came to the wood pile and he found a hole and crawled into it. His wrist was swelling and bruising where she had struck it with the wood, and he cried so hard his heart felt like it was bursting.

"God," he said as he sobbed and choked, "please, God. Tell my mom that I didn't do that. Tell my mom that I didn't do those things. They made me—she made me. I'm just a kid and she's bigger and I'm sorry, and Mama won't listen."

Arthur didn't understand how this could happen. His sister stole money from her parents, she lied, she ran away from home all the time, she accused Joe of molesting her—she did it all. And his sister and his brother, they were at the house and they weren't in trouble. They were older and they weren't punished. And Arthur didn't understand.

"God, please," he prayed. "Mama won't listen to me, but you know and she listens to you. Tell her, I didn't do those things."

❧ ❖ ☙

Parents make mistakes and children pay the price.

PART THREE

THE TRAIL

It's really cold now. I'm crouching down in the snow with my arms around my legs to warm them up. Thank God there is not much wind tonight and now the skin on my face is so numb. What little breeze there is shoots ice pellets painfully into my eyes. I think I have walked maybe two miles and so I'm half way to the camp. Walking a mile on frozen truck tracks in the snow is like walking three miles. My calves hurt and my ankles keep giving out even though I have boots that give them support. I don't like stopping, but these jeans are frozen stiff like a board and the skin on my legs is so cold I can't feel it.

Okay, I'm scared.

As I crouch here, I feel like I'm being watched from something in the trees. The hair on my neck stands up. I listen to the silence being interrupted with the occasional pop from the tree branches freezing. I rub my legs with my hands and then blow down the neck of my jacket to warm up. I have matches and later, if I need to, I can make a fire to get warm.

I stand up and listen. I'm hoping to hear a truck engine, hoping that someone else is stupid like us and is going into camp on Sunday night. But there's no engine, just the hiss of the treetops playing with the breeze.

I start walking again, putting my hands under my arms for a while to try and protect them. It would be awful to lose my fingers.

I'm in real danger now, Son. I have to make a decision. Do I try to walk the next two miles to camp or do I walk back to the car? I'm not sure I will make it two miles no matter which direction I go. I'm so cold now I'm really worried I'm going to freeze to death out here. If I go to the camp and make it, there will be shelter and food and a stove. If I go back to the car there will be my half-frozen brother, unless I drop before getting to the car. How sad is that? Me—going back with my tail between my legs and then freezing to death feet away from the car.

I keep walking to the camp and then I think—what if the trucker is wrong and the camp is six miles or even farther?

"Well," I say out loud. "I don't think I can make another two miles so it doesn't matter if the camp is more than that, I will die anyway. But there is a chance the trucker was wrong and the camp is only around this next curve, or the one after that." I want to smile but my face can't move.

I'm so cold now. I put my mouth under my collar and blow out. My breath helps to warm me. I breathe in through my nose and every breath stabs my lungs. I look up at the sky for clouds, but the icy wind is making my eyes water, blurring my vision. The stars, they shine ice-bright against the night sky, Son. They are beautiful…

A shiver races down my back and I can feel the cold entering deep under my skin. I hunch down, close to the ground, and wrap my arms around my legs for a minute. As time goes by the pain lessens and my eyes, they feel so heavy and I let them drift closed.

A wolf howls.

My eyes fly open and I struggle to stand on legs that do not want to move. I stagger forward a few steps like an old, arthritic man until the muscles start to loosen up. The wolves are too close, I can feel them. It's suicide to give them a reason to think I am done. I swear under my breath at how stupid I am for being like this, stuck in the cold. I swallow hard and resist the urge to lick my numb lips. I am so thirsty. I know better, me, than to eat the snow. It will make me colder on the inside. If I had been prepared, I would have a bottle of water under my coat to keep it from freezing. If I had been prepared, I wouldn't be out here walking in the first place.

"Tabarnak!"

The snow is crunching crisply under my boots with a crust that makes the way hard for my feet. I step on snow that's almost hard enough to hold my weight—almost. It breaks and my knee jars when my leg falls through and as I fall forward the icy snow cuts and it—oh, how you say—irriter—how you say in English? It rubs. Although, there is little feeling now. Before it really hurt; now, not so much. Now I feel the burn of my fingers and the way frozen jeans sound loud against the dark silence.

Arthur as a young man.

Arthur and his mother, Berthe.

CHAPTER SIXTEEN

THE BUNKER

If there was a strong wind or a storm, Arthur was also afraid a tornado was coming and would hit the house. In his mind he could see the house flying into the air—like the Wizard of Oz.

Arthur took a shovel and decided to shovel around the house. Why shoveling around the house would stop a tornado, he didn't know what, he just needed to do something? All it did was make Joe mad and then he had to fix the holes he dug and make sure he stayed out of reach of Joe's hands or duck if he took a swing at him.

It was 1962 when the family got their first black and white television. Arthur was 13 years old. He'd never seen one before, neither had his parents. They loved all of it, the news, commercials, it didn't matter what was on, they watched it all.

They especially loved watching Wagon Train, a show with lots of cowboys. There was an actor named Robert Fuller who they really love and also Terry Wilson who played Bill Hawks. Well, during one of the episodes they killed somebody. Arthur and Joe and his siblings watched mortified as this man died on the screen. Then the picture changed and a commercial came on.

"Look," says Arthur's dad as he jumps up from his chair. "He's not dead, he's eating cake."

That was the time of the cold war, and most of the news revolved around nuclear bombs and the issues between Russia and the United States. The world was afraid of nuclear war. People built bunkers against nuclear fallout. This all came to a climax in October of 1963, during the Cuban missile crisis. Everyone was worried that Russia would drop bombs on the United States and because St. Labre was so close to the border the fall-out would be horrible. So, the Nuns taught the kids in St. Labre School to duck and cover. There were drills where the Nun would blow a whistle and all the kids would duck under their desks and cover their heads with their arms. They were taught that the people in the bigger cities in the U.S. were building bunkers underground, so they could survive closer to the bomb sites.

Arthur was taught to duck and cover just like the other kids, but he realized that during a nuclear war ducking and covering wasn't enough. He worried that he was going to die, if there was a nuclear bomb. At school the Nuns seemed to know what to do, and so he felt safe there. But at home, he didn't know what would happen. Where would he hide?

He figured that he could do better than hiding under a bench or a desk. He got a shovel and dug a really big hole in the ground, then put stuff on top, like dirt and grass and twigs. Only one bunker wasn't enough, since he would be too far away to get into it if there was a bomb. He needed lots of bunkers for himself and for his whole family and in places close to where they might be working as well as close to the house.

He dug a really big bunker by the pig pen and put twigs over it, then dirt and some grass. It was really well hidden and Arthur was satisfied it would keep them safe from the atomic bomb.

It was threshing time at home. Every day, Joe drove this big McCormick tractor pulling the thresher, back and forth through the yard. Coming in for the night, he drove that McCormick tractor right towards the bunker. Arthur saw him coming and waved his arms and yelled and held his breath and prayed as he watched in horror. The tractor drives up to the pig pen, then just about past it. Arthur is starting to think the tractor missed the bunker when bang—the back wheel of that big McCormick falls into that bunker. Joe didn't need to wonder which one of his nineteen kids dug that hole.

"Arthur," he yelled and the pigs started screaming and squealing. "Tabernak! You are the stupidest kid! When I get my hands on you, I'm going to kill you…"

He was mad. The pigs screamed and Joe yelled at Arthur to feed the pigs to shut them up while he's trying to figure out how to get the tractor out of the hole and Arthur's afraid to go past him to feed the pigs because he's yelling that he's going to kill him. Norbert was rolling on the ground and laughing, but not Arthur, he was too busy ducking and trying to keep away from Joe's big hands.

Arthur's best friend in the whole world was Norbert. The two were best friends, not just brothers. Arthur could talk to Norbert and the two of them held on tight to each other's secrets. The biggest shock of Arthur's life was the next day when he got home from school. Norbert wasn't there when they all sat down for supper.

"Mama, where's Norbert?"

"Do you have homework tonight?" She said.

"Yes, I've always got homework. School is stupid, they don't teach me nothing. Where is he, Mama? Where is Norbert?" Berthe looked upset, and Joe spoke up.

"Norbert is sick, Arthur. He has trouble sleeping at night. We took him to the doctor in Winnipeg today and the doctor put him in a special hospital for people like him. They are going to make him better. Now shut-up and eat."

"When will he be home?" Asked Arthur.

"Not for a long time. Maybe even a year," Berthe said. "When he comes home, he will be his old self again, he'll be even better than that. You'll see."

"He's in a mental institute. They just dropped him off there," said one of his brothers.

"If you don't shut-up and eat we'll drop you there next," yelled Joe.

"You better behave Arthur; you give Mama the most trouble," said one of his brothers in bed that night.

"Do not," said Arthur. Inside, he was scared, really scared. Norbert was his only friend; without him, he was really alone.

'Am I next?' he thought to himself. *'Why did they do that to Norbert? If I'm too hard to deal with would they really do that to me too?'* Norbert was never the same after he came back from the institution.

Another brother was also sent to a similar mental institution in Portage la Prairie, at the age of twelve. When Arthur was sixteen or so, he visited him there. All the patients around him were mentally deranged and my brother was very sad and looked pitiful. He started walking with him and when they met two men dressed in white gowns, he immediately told Arthur to stop talking and keep on walking.

Arthur promised to return him to the institution after their walk but instead he took him with him in his car. They returned home to St. Labre and when they arrived, Arthur's mom immediately told Arthur "to mind his own business." His brother was later returned to the institution in Portage la Prairie. He had been sexually abused by people working there but unfortunately, I did not report that to my mother when I brought him back home. It might have changed her decision to return him to that hell hole. Neither brothers deserved to be in a mental institution.

❧❖❧

**Evaluate the good and bad things in your life.
Leave the bad parts behind you.**

CHAPTER SEVENTEEN

CHORES

Joe expected more from the boys than he did from the girls. Boys needed to work and work hard. He expected them to do a man's job and lost patience quickly when they didn't perform the way he wanted them to. An ongoing job was firewood. The house had a stove for heat and a smaller stove for cooking. This meant there had to be two wood piles. One had longer pieces for the large wood stove and the other shorter.

The boy's main job was to help with the firewood. The older ones cut down trees and took off the branches. The middle-aged kids, who were too young for the chainsaw, were expected to stack the firewood.

Joe yelled and cursed and swore to keep the kids working. If they didn't listen and they were too far away to cuff, he'd pick up whatever was close—usually a piece of firewood. He had great aim. All the kids heard was the wind whistling and a thud.

It wasn't always firewood he threw. Once he grabbed a shovel and threw it with his usual precision. The flat side hit the boy in the head and blood gushed everywhere. The child got up and ran off into the bush to a neighbor's house. The police arrived a short time later and Berthe answered the door.

"We have a report of child abuse, Ma'am," said the officer. "We need to speak to your husband about hitting his son on the head with a shovel?"

"He doesn't speak English—Joe," she calls and tells him why the police are at the door.

"My husband says the boy was playing and fell on a shovel," lied Berthe. She knew if she told the truth that Joe's anger would explode and she was afraid of what he would do to the boy, and to her. She didn't think anyone could protect them from Joe when he was angry. "He was supposed to be doing his chores and he ran off because he knew he'd be in trouble for fooling around when he was supposed to be working. Joe wasn't even home when it happened. He was in the bush."

The police continued to question them, but they both denied what happened.

"You tell him, if I ever come back here," the officer looked Joe in the eyes and pointed his finger at him as he spoke, "he's coming with me."

Arthur's brother came home with a bandage on his head. Joe pouted for half a year. He would leave in the morning and stay away all day.

"We don't own our kids," he told his brother-in-law, "We can't do what we want." He really resented the interference. But it had scared him and things were a little different after that. He'd still cuff them across their head and he continued to yell and call them names, saying they were good for nothing.

Arthur's thirteenth birthday was one of his happiest—Norbert came home. He was different than what Arthur remembered—expected. He spoke very slowly and was more serious about things. He seemed older, but it didn't matter, Arthur had missed him and he was so happy Norbert had come home.

"What was it like?" asked Arthur.

"Um—awful."

"What did you do there; did you get lots to eat?"

"Yes, there was lots to eat, and we got slippers and shoes and clothes, but I missed things like deer meat and rabbit stew. Mama makes the best rabbit stew. Mostly I stayed inside."

"I don't know why they did that. You were fine before."

"I'm home now, so I don't want to talk about it. I want to forget it."

Thirteen years old and Arthur was doing the work of a full-grown man. Things like emptying the crap bucket and milking the cows or gathering eggs, they were left for the girls and the younger kids. Arthur worked with Joe and the older boys in the bush, and haying, threshing, and clearing land.

"You stupid pile of horse shit!" He'd yell at them. They would duck automatically because usually he threw things at them when he yelled.

The haying was a family affair. The younger kids would have to sit on the top of the hay in the wagon to weigh it down. There weren't enough shoes for all of them so many were barefooted and while the soles of their feet were like shoe-leather, there were still many nights of picking hay slivers out of the feet, legs, hands or arms. The hay was filled with thistles and worse, sometimes poison ivy. Under the big toe the skin usually dried and then cracked and bled. A thorn would get in there and get infected. It was almost too sore to walk on, but it didn't matter. Joe made them work.

Arthur and Norbert would sit opposite to each other and put their feet on the other's lap. They would scratch each other's feet and it would feel so good they would scratch the skin off and it would get raw and hurt and would still itch from the poison ivy. They didn't have any medicine against poison ivy; or a bathtub to soak in. Sometimes they would run off to the creek after the day of work was done, but without shoes they would get more poison ivy and the horseflies would take chunks out of their skin unless they were totally immersed in the water.

The creek—in dry weather—was no more than a slough with thick, green sludge on the top and squishy, smelly mud at the bottom.

To hide from the bugs the boys would go under the water and come back up with handfuls of that slimy mud and smear it all over their bodies and all through their hair. It was cool and helped take the sting out of the poison ivy and the horseflies couldn't get through the mud to the skin. The deer flies and mosquitoes would try to fly up their nostrils, but they could deal with that. It wasn't perfect, but it helped. Of course, they couldn't wash off all the mud after, they cleaned up as best as they could before going to bed.

At night they would hide under blankets to keep the hordes of bloodthirsty mosquitoes from biting them and because they could not open the windows due to the lack of screens, the heat in the upstairs bedrooms made the rashes itch and sting. It was like that, night after night, no fresh air to breathe and no respite from the heat, either. After an almost sleepless night they would be up with the sun to do their chores and then back into the hay field until it was all done. The haying—not the work.

Haying caused Arthur further hardship. As a small boy, Arthur had hay fever every summer. His nose was either plugged or running so much that he had to try to "snort" the phlegm back down his throat. He constantly had to clear his throat and he made so much noise that everyone said "stop snorting". It was disgusting to the people around him, not to mention what Arthur had to endure. When he got fed up of always clearing up his throat or spitting it out, he would just hang his head and let the phlegm drip from his nose. Joe would tell Arthur, "stop snorting".

"I can't," Arthur would say. "My nose is leaking."

"Go wipe it on the grass," yelled Joe.

They had two horses on the farm. The horses were well looked after and used for hauling wood and pulling the cultivator. Joe was impatient with them sometimes. He'd push them and there was a battle of wills, especially with the male horse. Passing the cultivator over the field once, the male horse decided he wasn't going to do any more. Joe was whipping him and yelling, and the horse went crazy— up on his hind legs and pawing the air—then took off running for the barn with Joe running behind yelling for Arthur to stop the horse. Arthur ran out in front of the horse and started waving his hands because Joe told him to. He saw that horse galloping all out for the barn and realized there was no way that horse would stop. Arthur knew his dad would be really mad if he didn't stop the horse, but he knew that horse was going to hurt him if he tried to stop him, so Arthur moved well away from the horse. He was lucky he moved. The horse was still hitched up to the cultivator and if he had tried to stop the horse he would have been hit and killed by the cultivator.

Arthur was strong for his age and Norbert too. They went into the bush to cut firewood. Sometimes the tree was too heavy to lift up, Norbert and Joe would be on the big end and Arthur on the small end. Arthur lifted up the small end on his own but the other two couldn't budge the big end.

"Hey, you two weaklings," said Arthur. "You come to the small end and I'll lift the big end all by myself. You just see if I don't."

That's exactly what he did, and Joe and Norbert still couldn't lift up the small end—of course they didn't realize that when Arthur picked up the heavy end the small end got all the weight.

At the age of fourteen years old, Arthur's in the bush. He's carrying a 620-Pioneer chainsaw, and it is heavy. He's with his three older brothers. Arthur is falling the tree. He's cutting across in a line on the trunk of the tree so it falls on a stump and not on the ground so the boys can take blades and strip off the bark and branches. Tree after tree, he kept holding that chainsaw and cutting down trees until his arms were too tired to hold the saw. It was hard work and Joe expected them to work like that.

After a long day, Arthur's arm was really aching and he wanted to take a break. It was getting dark and Joe insisted in cutting a couple more trees before calling it a night. Arthur started up the saw but his arm was so tired it couldn't hold up the saw anymore and it dropped and cut into his leg. He needed stitches; the cut was long and deep and wouldn't stop bleeding. Joe told Berthe to wrap it tightly and he'd be fine. He added that she should put a picture of the

Holy Mother and it would help heal faster. He didn't want to take time away from work to drive Arthur to the hospital for stitches.

The winter was the best time for cutting wood. It was cold and there was the ice and snow to deal with, but there were no mosquitoes and horseflies. The leaves were gone off the trees too, which made them easier to strip. They used the horses to pull the logs out of the bush. The horses worked hard and really sweat. After a long day, they would walk the horses to the barn and the boys would take their two blankets off their bed and dry off the horses so they wouldn't freeze overnight. There weren't any spare blankets, so the damp ones used for the horses had to be taken back upstairs and used to cover the boys at night.

Even today, when a family member talks about a warm, nice blanket they owned when they were young, Arthur still feels a pang of jealousy because he never had that in his youth.

❦❖❧

Don't give your power away!

CHAPTER EIGHTEEN

CHANGES

Joe, Norbert and Arthur were working on a homemade trailer, made with the frame of an old truck to which you added a metal bar to attach to a tractor. Arthur was underneath holding a bolt and the other two were doing something on top. Arthur was lying on his back and he could see Norbert above him through a little hole. The two of them started laughing at each other and Joe was getting mad.

"Câlice! You idiots," he yelled at them and cuffed Norbert across the head. Joe then got off the wagon to get something and told Norbert to keep holding the clamp in place. Arthur and Norbert started laughing again.

"Shut-up, you little bastards," he yelled and started to kick at Arthur, kicked him in the head and on his arms and legs as he yelled. Over and over he kicked him.

Norbert and Arthur worked all day with Joe. After the trailer, they went into the bush for the afternoon to cut wood. It was a long day; they ate supper late. Sitting at the table, Arthur was too sore to move. Joe pushed back his chair and opened the tin of tobacco. He rolled a smoke and lit it. Arthur and Norbert looked at each other and smiled. They both thought Joe was going to tell a story.

"Norbert," Joe said. "You are too old to be at home. You need to leave now."

No one said a word. Berthe had her back to the table and she didn't turn around, just continued doing the dishes with one of the older girls.

Joe takes a long drag on the cigarette and looks at Norbert.

"Did you hear me? You need to leave the house. Right now—gather your things and get out."

"Papa," Norbert said, "Where do I go? It's 10 o'clock and dark outside. Can I leave in the morning so I can find a place to sleep?"

"No," said Joe. "Get out."

Norbert stood up and, on his way out said to Joe, "Watch what will happen to you tonight." A threat like Joe used on his kids all their life. Norbert went to stay with a neighbor who was a bachelor and was happy for the help and the company.

Arthur went to bed and laid there after Norbert left, worrying *Where did he go?'* He felt so sad for his brother. He cried himself to sleep that night. He was his helpmate all summer in the bush. Now it was late fall and Joe didn't need Norbert anymore and he was throwing him out like you do an old rag.

∼❖∽

Love liberates you. It does not bind you!

CHAPTER NINETEEN

THE FIGHT

Anger—pure unadulterated anger is how Arthur felt and useless too.

Arthur missed Norbert, although Norbert still came by the house and helped with wood and various jobs, it wasn't the same.

Everyday Arthur went to school. He was 15 and in grade four. He still couldn't read or write. He never passed grade 3. He only passed grade two by the skin of his teeth. The nuns got him to clear the sidewalk in the winter, mop the floors of the hallway, and many other jobs around the school. He still didn't know how to read or write. The nuns didn't know what to do with him any longer and moved him forward to grade four so he wouldn't be with the littlest kids. Arthur thought it was a big joke—a big useless joke.

Arthur stopped bringing homework home. He gave up.

The nuns think I'm stupid, Papa calls me stupid and I couldn't learn anything at school—they must be right—I'm stupid,' he thought to himself.

"Where is your homework, Arthur?"

"I'm not doing homework anymore, Papa," said Arthur. "I am not bringing homework home. You can beat me up, you can kick me or hit me in the head, you can do what you want but I am not bringing homework home." Joe beat him and left him outside to think about things. Joe's words were as good as chains. Arthur stayed outside until he was given permission to come back into the house.

The next day Arthur came home without any homework and the day after and the day after that. Everyday Joe beat him—smacked him back and forth across the head and anywhere else he could reach until he figured Arthur had had enough. It didn't matter. Arthur refused to bring homework home.

Joe gave up. The tension between them didn't, though. It grew worse. They argued about everything and Joe yelled and called him names continually.

"You are stupid, Arthur. You are ugly and stupid, the worst kid I have," Joe yelled at him when they were in the barn. "When you are 16 you are out of here—gone—and I don't want to see you again."

Arthur was quiet. He simply looked at his dad. Joe looked back.

"If you don't want to see me, then why did you make me?"

Joe exploded. He grabbed Arthur and threw him across the barn, kicked him and grabbed him and threw him back the other way, from one end to the other.

"I didn't know I was creating a cow like you," he yelled and dragged him through all the cow manure. "If I had known how you were going to turn out I wouldn't have made you at all. You are worse than stupid—you are a useless piece of shit. Good for nothing. That's what you are, stupid and good for nothing!" he kicked him over and over.

The next day, bruised and beaten, Arthur refused to go to school at all. He worked on the farm and did chores day after day, but did not return to school. At night, to keep out of Joe's way, he went to the neighbors' and hung around with his cousin Bill. Joe didn't want Arthur to go there, he was afraid the rest of the family would find out that Arthur was not going to school anymore. Arthur ignored him and went anyway.

"Get out of here," Joe screamed at him. "You're no good—you're more trouble than you're worth and this is not your home anymore."

Berthe sat there at the table and didn't say a word. Arthur looked at her for support, but she didn't look at Arthur at all. Finally, his mother said "I want you to leave too".

'This is her idea,' he thought to himself. *'She never liked me, she hated me. And now she wants Papa to throw me out. She's happy I'm leaving.'*

Fifteen-year-old Arthur didn't say a word. Even though Arthur worked so hard he always felt like he was not wanted in his own home. At the table, in bed, any place he did not feel wanted. *I'm disgusting to them.* He left. It was dark outside; early fall with the smell of snow in the air and heavy frost most mornings. Arthur took an axe with him, the rifle he had saved up for and bought and his winter coat and boots.

That was all he owned and he had nowhere to go.

Later, when he turned sixteen, he went to Prince George, BC. He kept remembering what his mother had said and every time it made him cry. It did not matter where he was, he always cried when he thought of this. But, no matter how depressed Arthur was, he did not resort to alcohol or drugs to numb the pain. He always wanted to stay sober and alert. He had to be in control of himself and knew that he had to stay away from alcohol and drugs. He didn't want to do things he would regret the next day. He remembered what it had done to one of his older brothers who was so stoned once when cutting wood with him, he was hugging the tree instead of cutting it down. He never wanted to be that way.

❧ ❖ ☙

**Time doesn't wait for you!
Grab the opportunity when it's offered to you.**

PART FOUR

THE TRAIL

I'm certain I have walked four miles—but there is no camp in sight. The trucker wasn't telling the truth or maybe he was guessing. I'm so cold I am shaking and my legs are like wood. I keep my hands under my arms, but even they have no feeling.

I stop and crouch in the snow again. I wrap my arms around my legs and there is no heat. Then I remember the matches. I look around and see some dry moss on some branches, but I got no paper. I take out the matches anyway, but my hands are shaking too much—my shivers so violent—I can't light a match. I waited too long to build a fire that would save me. This is the coldest I've ever been in my life and man, I've been cold but this is the worst. I am freezing and I thought at the beginning of this walk that *hey, if I get cold I can go in the bush and make a fire. I have matches on me and everything.* Then I wait too long and I can't use them. I should have built a fire sooner—I should have brought water—I should have stayed in the car—I should have stayed in Winnipeg and drove into camp in the morning.

I can't turn around now, I have walked too far. I have to keep moving for as long as I can hoping that around this next corner I will find the camp.

I look up at the night sky, at the stars, glittering above me. But wait. I see something strange. I see the trees move—their shadows are changing colour—maybe I'm close to death. In their branches I see them black, then green, then black once again. In the distance I hear a howl and I know that somewhere the wolves are sensing my death. They don't need to attack me, they will save their strength and follow me and wait.

"I won't go easy," my voice sounds like sand paper grinding metal. "Stay back, I won't let you win."

If I can make it around that next corner up there—that's where the camp will be—just a few more yards—it's there—it has to be...

No camp, Son. There must be another bend up ahead, only I can't see one. Okay, I can barely see the trail. My eyelashes are so thick with ice I can't see out of the corners, I have to look straight on. I rub them and the ice pulls at the lashes and makes my eyes water. I feel the tears run down my cheeks—a warm stream—until it freezes to my skin.

I'm now getting scared for my legs. I'm thinking, *if I make it at all, if my legs are frozen then they'll have to cut them off.* All I can do, and I do it often, is crouch on my legs and my legs, they are frozen. I try to rub them but there is nothing I can do. They are frozen and now I'm starting to think about this—I'm going to die on this road. Nobody's coming and I'm going to die on this road. I can feel the panic inside. I'm in real trouble.

I wonder what my Papa would say to me if he saw me out here like this. He'd probably say he always knew I was stupid. My whole family, son, they told me I was ugly and stupid. I always believed them, I mean—my goodness. They were my family, shouldn't they know?

Son, I'm so glad you are here with me. If I never had a son, then I would die alone...

I stumble forward and get to the next bend, but there is only the trail and the bush. So I say again to myself as I walk, *keep going, just to the next corner, it has to be there. The camp will be there.* I start thinking about my family. I think about my brothers and sisters and my kids. So you know, and things that I own and what I was going to do—my plans. I can't go back and warn any of you about anything. Death is facing me; right in my face. Either the animals are going to eat me or I'll freeze to death—I know one of those things is going to happen. Unless the camp is there… and there's a curve there and I know the camp is just around the corner. I get to the corner, but it isn't and up ahead there is another curve and I am worried. I'm panicking.

I move my feet forward. The jeans bend, but I can't feel them against my legs. My feet are blocks of ice. There is no wind down low, but the trees whisper above. Sometimes there is a snap. Is it a foot breaking a stick? Or is it a frozen tree popping? I swivel around, but there's nothing there—if you can say a frozen man in two pairs of frozen jeans can swivel, then I guess I may have swiveled.

Son, I am shaking so hard I'm almost falling over. I want to sleep; rest my eyes for just a moment; pull my hands in and curl up in the snow long enough to get warm. I know better, me. I know the bush, but I forgot that the bush knows me.

CHAPTER TWENTY

KICKED OUT

"*I could have cleaned his clock so fast that his head would spin—but I can't revenge on my Papa. This was Mama—she did this,*' Arthur thought to himself. In his mind he still saw her face while she sat at the table and said nothing. She was his Mama and she betrayed him, it had to have been her.

There was nowhere to go. He was too embarrassed to go to an aunt or an uncle.

Arthur looked up at the sky. It was cold but clear and the stars were bright against the blackness. He sighed and walked across the field, not even a quarter of a mile to the old camp—where a small clapboard building stood for hunters.

'*All the other kids had to leave home when they reached 16 because the family allowance didn't pay for them anymore. We are only worth $5 a month to my parents. But me? I'm worth less. They didn't even keep me until I was 16*', he thought to himself as he walked alone across the field to his new home.

Arthur pulled open the broken door and went inside. He lit a match and looked around. It was only one room, with a broken window in the back and another broken window in the front with cardboard blocking the holes. There was an old bunk bed in one corner and a wood stove and a table and that was it. No toilet—not even an outhouse—but he was used to that.

In one corner there was a hole in the bare wood floor; access to a dirt cellar.

There was this man, Etienne, he got lost and everyone around went looking for him in the bush—over a hundred people searched. After three days they gave up. The last person to see him was Joe, who saw him leaning against the wall at the camp with a man named Dupuis, who was living at the camp. Joe saw Etienne go into the building with Dupuis, but didn't see him come out again. He didn't think anything of it.

Years later, when Arthur's older brother was kicked out, he lived at the camp too. He dug under the building to make a dirt cellar to store some potatoes and he found the bones. He called the RCMP, but they never came.

The boys believed the camp was haunted and used to make up ghost stories to scare the little kids.

Now it was Arthur's new home.

The first night he was terrified and cold. It was black inside the shack. It didn't have electricity so he sat alone in the dark. Arthur hadn't brought a lantern or even a flashlight—just matches. The wood stove was useless since Arthur didn't have paper or wood.

All he had was the money he had saved in the tobacco tin buried in the yard. He walked to the store the next day and bought bread and some cheese whiz and started an account.

"I've left home, Uncle," explained Arthur. "I'm living at the old hunter's camp. I'll pay you when I get some work."

"That will be fine."

Norbert came to find him and a couple of other brothers. They helped him cut wood, which they stacked along one wall. He made a fire and it was roasting hot in the small shack, but without it roaring he was really cold because it was fall and the air was damp. In a week the wood was gone.

Arthur pulled off the broken door and fixed it—sort of. He had a little money, but not enough. He thought about trying to get work in Winnipeg, but he didn't know how to get there. He didn't speak English, other than *hello* and maybe *how are you*. He couldn't read or write. He didn't even know the way to Woodridge, or Steinbach. It was a lonely, rejected existence. He was an Adam, but no longer lived with the family. He didn't feel grown up, he felt young—a kid. It was not a happy place to be. How can parents have kids and not give them the basic knowledge needed to make it in life? Arthur's parents did that to him. He did not know anything about life outside the Adam home.

Snow could come anytime and he worried about the winter. The shack had thin walls and he didn't know if he could get enough wood to last, or anything else he needed for winter unless he stole it. He was terrified—almost paralyzed with fear.

"Stay with me," Arthur told Norbert when he came to visit.

"Okay, I'll stay with you," he said.

Arthur ran up a tab of $20, which was a lot of money. Norbert did the same thing. They couldn't pay it and the Uncle yelled at them when they came into the store.

"You owe me money, the both of you. You have to pay, no more charging." Norbert started to laugh and then Arthur laughed. Their uncle went red in the face.

"You stop laughing you or I'll get the baseball bat and hit you over the head," They both took off running.

One night after church, it's dark and the boys are walking back to the camp and pass by their Uncle's store. Along the side of the building in a wooden lean-to there were empty glass bottles, which are worth two cents each. They decide to steal 6 each.

Their Uncle was upstairs and happened to see their shadows from the window, but can't see who it is. He hears the clinking of glass and he knows someone is trying to steal his empties and opens the window.

"I hear you; you leave my empties alone. I'm getting my gun," he yells.

The boys dropped the bottles and started to run away.

"I'm not stealing anything," yelled Norbert.

"Norbert!" His uncle had recognized his voice. "I know that's you. Don't you ever step foot in my store again."

Arthur hadn't said a thing so he had to shop for both of them until their uncle forgave Norbert.

Norbert stayed with Arthur at the camp for a couple weeks and then he left and Arthur was alone again.

Arthur sat in the dark in the shack looking out the window at his home, seeing the lights and his family but he couldn't live there!

At first, he blamed himself. What had he done wrong for his mother and father to hate him so much? But the more he thought about it, he realized that the problem was not with him. He might be a bit of a hard one to handle at times, he did lie sometimes, and he stole things – but only because he had to survive. Deep down, he was a good kid, and with the proper guidance and love, especially love, he would do well in this world, even without an education. He was intelligent, smart, was good at figuring things out, resourceful, was not afraid of hard work, and most of all, he had a good heart. He wanted a good life and he would get it. You watch Arthur Adam go!! He'll be somebody some day!

You can not change something that you don't acknowledge!

"I can never revenge against my father,"
Arthur would later say about his relationship with Joe.

CHAPTER TWENTY-ONE

THE KINDNESS OF STRANGERS

Eventually, Arthur went by his parent's place and helped with chores and jobs Joe needed help with. He was given the occasional meal, but it was clear—it was no longer his home.

About a month after being kicked out, Arthur was walking down the road on the way to town—there was a fresh snowfall on the ground and it crunched under his boots. The air was alive with ice-crystals that glittered in the sun. It was the kind of morning he usually loved. Not today. He was destitute and lonely.

"Excusez-moi, s'il vous plait," (Excuse me please) A truck had pulled up beside him and a man was leaning out the window. "Bonjour, ca va?" he said in French.

"Oui, eh vous? (Yes, and you?)" replied Arthur.

"You look like you're from around here, I'm out here hunting. What are you doing?"

"Nothing," said Arthur. "I'm just going home."

"Is there any deer around?"

"Yeah," he said. "There's lots of deer. Do you want me to show you?"

"Yeah," he said.

"My name's Louis, I live in Lorette," he said when Arthur got in the truck.

Arthur took him down a back road and then Louis got his gun and they walked through the woods. They were chatting and while there were lots of deer out, Louis never took a shot.

Arthur said to him, "Would you have a job for me?"

"Don't you go to school?" he asked.

"No," he said. "I don't go to school."

"Well," he says. "What is your dad going to say?"

"I don't live with my dad. That camp with the shack where you stopped to talk to me—I live there and I don't have money to buy food so I'm looking for a job. I can cut firewood and I'm strong."

"How much do you want a day?" Arthur stopped walking and looked at Louis. He didn't know what to say. He had no idea how much a man made.

"Whatever you say," Arthur finally said. He had nothing, so anything was better than what he had. As it was, the man lived in Lorette. Arthur didn't know where that was. He'd have to make enough so he could find a place to live.

"Well, I'll give you $2 a day and room and board."

"Well, yeah," says Arthur and shakes the man's hand.

"But," said Louis, "I have to ask your dad if it's okay."

Louis drives Arthur back to his camp.

"I'll just go and get my stuff," says Arthur. He gets out and goes into the shack and looks around. Nothing. The only thing he wants to bring with him is his hunting rifle. Otherwise, there's nothing—there is nothing there—nothing.

Louis drives him to Joe and Berthe's. The pair walk into the house and Arthur introduces him to his parents.

"I want to take your son to work, is that okay?" Louis said to Joe,

"Yeah," says Joe. "That's fine."

'This kid has nothing to take with him but his rifle, no clothes—nothing and his parents—they don't even ask where I'm taking him or what he's being paid or where he'll live?' wondered Louis. What a heartless father!

Louis and Arthur talked all the way to Lorette. Arthur was excited. He felt good about himself and he really liked Louis. In Lorette, Louis turned off the main road and drove up a long driveway to a beautiful house.

Arthur stared.

They had a beautiful house. Louis' wife didn't seem surprised to meet him or bothered at all about him staying there. The only thing that bothered Arthur was the washroom. The door was being replaced so there was no door.

'Nobody's going to catch me in there, I'm in a strange house and there's no door on the toilet,' he thought to himself.

It was heaven to Arthur. He slept in a real bed with blankets and a pillow. It was warm and the food was amazing. On top of that, he could take a shower or a bath anytime he wanted. It was the first time in his life that he was able to take a bath in a bathtub.

"Hey you, Arthur," said Louis after a couple of days. "Where do you go to the toilet, you?"

Arthur didn't know what to say. If he thought Louis would believe he didn't go to the toilet at all, then he'd tell him that. But Arthur knew he wouldn't believe that.

"I go outside— in the bush," he said with a red face.

"Why don't you use the washroom in the house?"

"There's no door…" That weekend Louis gave Arthur the job of hanging the new door on the bathroom.

Sunday morning greeted Arthur with the smell of bacon and pancakes. Every morning he felt he was living a dream.

"Arthur," Louis said after breakfast, "You need to change so we can go to church."

Arthur didn't have anything to change into. He went upstairs and washed, combed his hair and went back downstairs.

"Didn't I tell you to change?" Louis is mad.

"I've got no clothes," said Arthur. "This is all I got."

Louis was quiet. He went to his wife and asked if their son would have something that would fit Arthur. After church, he took Arthur to Winnipeg and bought him some clothes.

Arthur worked for Louis in Lorette for the winter before going back to St. Labre.

❧❖☙

Rejoice in your accomplishments, but be humble.

CHAPTER TWENTY-TWO

ST. BONIFACE

When Arthur left Lorette, he went home and worked with the forestry for the spring. After living in a nice house and sleeping in a real bed, he was shocked at the place where he had grown up. His mother worked non-stop, but the house was filthy and with all those kids the noise was almost too much to bear. Arthur never remembered it that way and it made him sad.

A couple of weeks after his 16th birthday, Arthur went to St. Boniface to look for work. He went to the unemployment office. He didn't know that a lot of people in St. Boniface spoke French; he assumed they only spoke English.

"Me, job, farmer," Arthur said in English.

"Okay," said the counter clerk who checked a piece of paper and dialed the telephone. "Hey, I got a guy to work for you."

Arthur didn't want a job as a farmer; he was trying to tell the clerk where he came from.

"Go sit down over there," said the clerk pointing to some chairs against the wall. "Someone is coming to pick you up."

Arthur had arrived at 9 a.m. He fell asleep in the chair and at 2 p.m. someone shook his shoulder and was told to go with a person called "Guy".

Guy spoke English, and French. He took Arthur to his car and he got in. He didn't know where he was going, or what kind of work he would be doing. All he knew was this was his ride.

Guy drives through the city of Winnipeg and stops in front of a house. And he motions to Arthur to get out and come into the house with him. Guy is greeted by a young girl and kissed. Arthur figures out she's Guy's girlfriend.

Arthur is shown the couch and the two disappear into a bedroom in the back. Arthur sits down and falls asleep.

When Guy wakes Arthur up its dark outside. The two get back into Guy's car and continue driving out of Winnipeg. They end up in the town of Haywood and out on a farm. Arthur wasn't fond of farm work, but it was work and he was being paid and had a place to sleep and his boss, Marcel, spoke French.

"Do you have a sister named Teresa?" His boss asked him about a week after he started working there.

"Yeah,"

"She's lost in the bush. They're looking for her, it's on the news. Come listen to the radio."

There it was; Teresa Adam from St. Labre lost in the bush since Monday. And Arthur couldn't believe it. He felt sick. He knew he had to go and help look for her. He asked for a ride to Winnipeg and Guy took him to the highway where he got a ride with the St. Claude Transfer. Arthur only had $6 on him. He doesn't know the city at all. No one understands his French and he can't figure out how to get to St. Labre. He didn't even know which direction it was. He wrote down his Aunt's address and someone helped him find her.

Arthur arrives at his Aunt's house as she is leaving for church. She doesn't drive and she tells him they'll figure out a way to get him to St. Labre after church.

Sitting in the pew with his aunt, Arthur looks around at all the people. He needs to find meone who can speak French. He sees a man on the other side, and it looks like he's praying in French. Arthur watched him after the service and caught up with him outside.

"Excuse me. I am Arthur Adam,"

"Hello, my name is Gabriel Soulodre. What can I help you with young man?"

"My sister is lost in the bush in St. Labre and I don't know the way out of town and I don't have a car. Can you help me?"

Gabriel had heard of Teresa being lost in the bush. It was in the newspapers and all over the radio. He said, "No." because he didn't believe Arthur.

"Okay—thank you anyway," said Arthur. He didn't know what to do next. Maybe go and find someone who could tell him the way and he'd try to hitch-hike.

Gabriel watched the coarse and poorly dressed young man walk away. He recognized the older woman who joined him. Perhaps he was being hasty. Maybe this boy was being truthful.

Arthur and his aunt started walking towards her home a couple of blocks away. A big Pontiac slowed to a stop beside them. It's Gabriel. He says to my aunt,

"I'll help him out," he said to Arthur's Aunt, "hop in Arthur."

Gabriel drove him to the bus depot and purchased a ticket for him. The closest the bus went to St. Labre was about 20 miles away.

Arthur wanted to hug him, but stuck out his hand instead. Gabriel grabbed his hand and put a $2 bill in it and a piece of paper with his phone number on it.

"When you get back to Winnipeg, give me a call."

❧❖☙

Never forget the kindness of strangers.

CHAPTER TWENTY-THREE

THE SEARCH FOR THERESA

Arthur arrived home that evening. His mother was grief stricken and his father looked haggard.

'You should be upset, old man,' Arthur thought. *'You must have known this was bound to happen, all the times you sent little kids out into the bush chasing cows and picking berries—all alone.'*

The yard around the house was filled with vehicles; the house was crawling with people. Casseroles lined the counter, and cookies and baked goods. Thermoses of coffee were passed around as searchers came in to warm up. There was a huge bonfire in the yard and overhead a helicopter flew in large circles. More vehicles drove in with searchlights and a couple of big spot lights were shot into the air in case Teresa could see them. If she did, then maybe she'd walk towards them, if she could still walk.

The mood was sober. The first day there was so much hope. But going into the second night people were discouraged. The area was under water because of recent rain and while an odd footprint was found here and there, there wasn't enough evidence to go on. A dog was brought in, but also couldn't track her.

As darkness fell, many went home cold, wet, and filled with wood ticks and mosquito bites. All through the night, for miles, voices could be heard calling to Teresa.

"We're here," they called. "We aren't going to leave you alone in the dark honey. Be patient, we'll find you tomorrow." A group of people took turns calling all night for miles, hoping that Teresa was alive, and if so, she could hear them and hang on just one more night. It terrified everyone to think of a small nine-year-old girl lost and alone, wet and cold, in the bush in the dark. Hearts broke all over Southeastern Manitoba.

Soldiers from the 3rd Regiment, Royal Canadian Horse Artillery arrived at daybreak on Wednesday morning. It started to rain. The helicopter started circling as the soldiers fanned out in all directions.

"Teresa! Teresa!" They called and then waited for a couple of seconds to give her a chance to respond.

Arthur did some searching and returned to the house. He was worried about his mother. She was so upset. He watched her holding in the tears and he wanted to hug her and tell her it would be okay. But he didn't know how. He couldn't ever remember his mother hugging him—she must have though when he was young—when he was a baby, maybe? The only time he remembers any touching was in anger, and now, when he wanted to reach out and give her comfort, he didn't know how.

Two soldiers were searching and poking the ground with long sticks about a mile from the Adam farm. One of them thought he saw an oddly shaped lump of dirt between two logs and waved to the other one who knelt down and touched it. It was Teresa. She moved and opened her eyes. She was shivering and her skin was blue from the cold.

"We've found her! We got her!" They scooped her up in a blanket and carried her through the bush. She smiled at them.

"Thank you that you found," she said in broken English.

Searchers burst into the Adam's house yelling, "They found her, alive!" Berthe broke down, and Arthur ran outside to wait for his sister.

"They found her. Thank you, thank you everyone. We could

never ever repay you for all you have done for us," said one of Arthur's sisters. Teresa was taken by helicopter to the hospital along with her mother. Arthur stayed to help with the farm chores until his parents returned.

Joe had been searching in the bush when he heard. He arrived at the hospital just before 5 o'clock in the evening. He fought back the tears as he hugged his daughter.

"I heard people calling me, but I couldn't holler very loud," she told her parents. "I didn't sleep, eat or drink, but I wasn't scared. I was just so cold. I heard a rooster crow and cars, but I couldn't tell where they came from. I saw planes and the helicopter and I waved, but I couldn't stand up anymore."

Teresa and her brother and sister had been stripping bark in the bush not far from the farmhouse. Teresa decided to go home and wandered off at about dinner time. No one knew she was missing until the other two came home for supper.

"I know where the planer is, the one I used to take the bark off, daddy," she said to Joe. "I get it when I get home, don't worry, I won't forget."

Joe dodged a bullet, sending three little kids into the bush to work while he stayed at home. Arthur always knew someday it would happen, that one of his kids would get lost rounding up the cows or getting wood.

❧✧☙

**Find your purpose in life.
You cannot go anywhere unless
You know where you are going.**

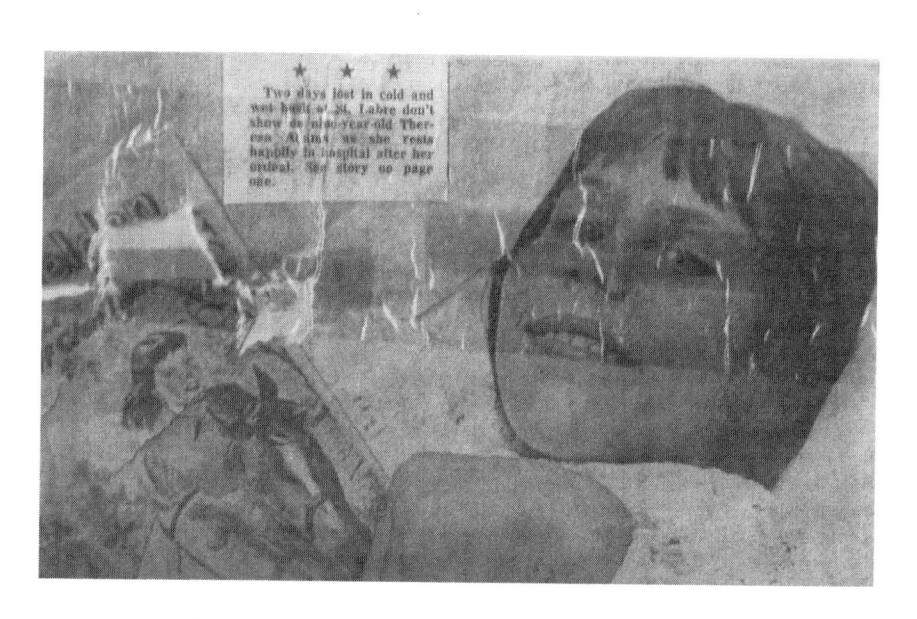

Theresa recovering in hospital after her ordeal.

CHAPTER TWENTY-FOUR

JIM

Arthur was out of money. He wandered around Winnipeg picking up odd jobs, but didn't really know what he was going to do. He didn't realize that there were people in the city that kept their eyes on young boys, and even though Arthur thought he was ugly—he wasn't. With his dark eyes and curly dark hair, he was tall and handsome.

Society was openly critical of anything 'different'. Women still struggled for equality as did minorities. Gays were openly targeted and despised for the most part. Arthur had never met a gay man.

One day Arthur was walking on Tache Avenue and out of money, as usual. He hears a car behind him and stops to look. He's wearing a long white coat floppy kind of thing. Anyway, this Cadillac pulls up beside him and this guy opens the door. His name is Jim, and asks Arthur if he needed a ride.

Arthur said sure and got in. He looked at Jim and was pretty sure he was gay. It made sense. A guy with an expensive car that drives down the road and asked a young teenage boy if he can give him a ride? Arthur is pretty tough and very sure he can look after himself, so he really didn't care if Jim was gay or not, a ride was a ride.

Arthur had been around English people enough lately that he

was learning to speak it fairly well.

"Nice Cadillac," He said and looked around.

"Thanks," Jim said.

Jim drove him where Arthur wanted to go and dropped him off without asking for anything.

A week or two after this, Arthur is out on his bicycle and Jim is cruising looking for him. Jim had been watching Arthur for a while and wanted to get to know him better. He saw Arthur on the bike and started to follow him.

Arthur rode through a stop sign and bang—was hit by a car. He heard the sound of the wheels of the car as it went over him. Jim and a couple of guys pulled him from under the car and up onto the sidewalk and waited for the police. Arthur is scratched up and his clothes are muddy and torn. An ambulance came and Arthur was taken to the hospital. It wasn't serious and they let him go.

Jim had followed the ambulance to the hospital and watched Arthur go into the Safeway a couple of blocks away. He went into the store and 'bumped' into him. He takes Arthur out to his car and gives him $3.

'I got nothing, I got no place to stay, I got nothing and he's such a nice guy. It's too bad he's queer. He's not touching me, but still.' Arthur thought to himself.

Arthur had been judged all his life. People judged him as a stupid Frenchman because he didn't read or write or speak very well. He didn't want to do the same thing to Jim, but he didn't know what to think.

Arthur thanked him for the money and Jim drove away and told his landlady about Arthur.

"He's just a young kid with no place to live, no education, doesn't speak English, no job and just got hit by a car." He told her.

"Go and find him, Jim. Bring him back here and we'll let him stay here—until he gets on his feet."

Jim finds Arthur and takes him home so he can get cleaned up. He washes Arthur's clothes and gives him some more money and something to eat. And this is how their friendship started—this went on for years. He never tried to touch Arthur or do anything to him. The only thing was that Jim couldn't keep his eyes off Arthur. It would make Arthur so mad because people saw Jim looking at him. Arthur would say "Stop looking at me!"

So, he stayed with him. And sometimes there'd be some kids around and Arthur never put it together about what was going on, because Jim never crossed the line with him.

Jim had a carpet cleaning business and asked Arthur to be his partner. It wasn't what Arthur wanted for his life, but he also didn't really know what he did want for his life. So, he and Jim became partners.

Business did so well; he helped Arthur find a suite and paid for it until he could make enough to pay for it himself. Jim picked him up every morning for work. He had his own key, and sometimes he would bring Arthur some food. The only thing that bothered Arthur was how Jim got jealous if he looked at girls—which he did all the time. They stayed friends for years, even after Arthur married and had children.

❧✧☙

Never judge a book by its cover.

Arthur with his son Darren.

CHAPTER TWENTY-FIVE

DRIVERS LICENSE

Arthur needed a driver's license. He had been driving for a couple of years, but he didn't have one. The trouble was, Arthur was only 17 and he couldn't get one until he was eighteen years old. He didn't know how he could do it, since he didn't read or write and only spoke French. You had no choice; you needed to read and write to do the written test.

"Go and get my license for me," he told his older brother. "Tell them you are Arthur Adam and that I am 18 – and never mind, I am not 18, you. Tell them you are 18."

Arthur had a plan. It was easier to get your driver's license in Steinbach because it's a small town and there are lots of farmers and immigrants there who have trouble with English. All Arthur needed was to get his license in Steinbach and then change the address to Winnipeg.

Arthur's brother had grade five. So, he passed the test without a problem. They take his photo for the license, which is fine because he and Arthur look similar enough.

Arthur gets that license and thinks he's king of the road, racking up six speeding tickets in a short time and he loses his license.

Arthur has to go in and take the test, and this time it's oral because he already had passed the written—at least his brother did.

He was a bit arrogant and didn't study the book. He figured why? He'd been driving so he knows the answers.

Arthur sits down with the driving instructor and the instructor starts asking questions like 'What do you do when you come to a red light?' Easy stuff.

"Okay," says the instructor. "You are going down the highway and it's stormy and you see a sign but you can't make out what it says what do you do?"

Arthur thinks to himself, *'Okay—I'd slow down. But that can't be it! That's too easy.'*

Arthur looks at the instructor and says: "Well, I usually carry a ladder with me in the back of the truck, so I would pull up to the sign, stop, put the ladder up against the sign, climb up the ladder to the sign, wipe it, look at it, climb back down the ladder and get into the truck and take off." And he smiles. He knows he answered right.

"No," Laughed the instructor, "no, no. The answer is slow down."

The next step was the driving test with the instructor in the truck with him.

'I'm a good driver,' Arthur thinks to himself, *'I'll get this easy.'*

The instructor gets in the truck and Arthur has the window down and his elbow out. *'Okay,'* He thinks to himself, *'the faster I drive the more I'm good'* and he takes off steering with one hand, comes to the corner and screeches around it, then boots it with spinning tires and the smell of rubber.

"Stop, let me off" the instructor yells and walks back to the office.

Arthur failed. He had to pay again.

"This time," the instructor looks at Arthur sternly, "you are going to drive the way I tell you to drive, both hands on the wheel, eyes on the road, no speeding, no squealing of tires, no taking corners on two wheels and... no burning rubber."

Arthur passed just like that.

A winner does things losers won't do, because it's easier for losers to do nothing.

CHAPTER TWENTY-SIX

PARENTS LOVE THEIR CHILDREN

Arthur bought himself a '57 Buick. He was out with friends one night at a discoteque called the Hungry Eye on Portage Avenue in Winnipeg. Most of them were drinking pretty heavily, except for Arthur—Arthur didn't really drink.

Arthur was asked to drive a guy named Teddy home as well as another buddy named Gene Walterson.

Teddy was drunk.

"Sure," said Arthur. "I'll drive him home. He's in Tuxedo, right? Gene, make sure he knows where we're going. He's so drunk he might not give us the right address."

After a couple of tries, they finally find the right address. It's 2 o'clock in the morning. Arthur parks and leaves Teddy with Gene. Teddy is out cold.

Arthur goes to the door and knocks. He's not sure he wants to be there waking up a guy so he can drag his drunk son into the house.

"Do you have a son named Teddy?" Arthur asks the man who answers the door, in his bathrobe.

"What do you mean, Teddy?" the man looks as though he's going to have a heart attack. "What is wrong with Teddy?"

"Nothing," said Arthur, "he's in my car, and he's drunk."

Teddy's dad runs down the sidewalk and yanks open the door. He's calling his son as he grabs him by the shirt and pulls him out. Leaning Teddy against the car, he taps his son gently on the cheeks.

"Why are you drunk, Teddy?" Teddy's dad puts his arm around his waist and helps him to the door.

"Thank you," he says to Arthur, "for bringing him home safely."

Arthur stood and watched.

'This man loves his kid,' he thought to himself. *'He really, really loves him.'*

Arthur was looking and seeing, but could not believe it. I didn't know that fathers love their kids that way.

Arthur got into the car and turned to Gene.

"That Teddy is one lucky guy. His dad really loves him. Me—every time I went past my dad, I ducked because I thought he was going to hit me." For years, every time Arthur saw men loving their sons, it hurt him.

It bothered Arthur for twenty years after that incident. He had never been loved like that.

❧ ✦ ☙

**Spend more time with your family.
You will never regret it.**

CHAPTER TWENTY-SEVEN

NEWDALE CONSTRUCTION

When Arthur was 17 he got a job at Stockyard Tire at a dollar an hour. He had been working on his English, and could manage to communicate fairly well. He didn't have a place to stay, and didn't have any money until he received his first pay cheque. He slept in cars. He walked down the street at night and tried the doors on parked cars until he found one that opened and slept there. He didn't have money for lunch, there wasn't anywhere he could wash regularly, and he ate whatever he could scrounge. On payday he rented himself a room.

Arthur kept working there while he looked for a better job with more pay. He wanted to drive heavy equipment. With so many boys at home he never learned to drive the tractor or the McCormick, but he really wanted to. He thought he'd be good at that.

Arthur heard that a company named Jensen Brothers were looking for someone who could drive a front-end loader. Arthur didn't know how to drive it. He didn't know anything about it. Nobody wanted to train someone, they wanted someone who was already trained and ready to work—Arthur needed training and decided if they weren't going to train him willingly, then he would have to get a job and learn quick.

Arthur applied for the job.

"So, Arthur," Said one of the Jensen brothers, "You can handle a front-end loader?"

"Sure," lied Arthur, "I got experience," he was ready for their next question.

"Where did you work?"

"For a company in Montreal," Arthur looked him right in the eye and didn't flinch.

"Can I have the name of the company?"

"Sure, but they're French and don't speak English. So, when you call make sure you have an interpreter." Arthur didn't want them to call, because the company in Montreal never heard of him. All he wanted was a chance.

Arthur wasn't the only one who applied. The Jensens decided to see how each of them did driving a Cat, and hire the best one for the job. Pierre, the other applicant, went first. Arthur looked at all the buttons and watched everything Pierre did. He watched how to start it, get it moving and doing things, what levers to work and buttons to push.

Arthur's turn came. He got into the cab like he lived there. The Cat jumped to life, and Arthur remembered how Pierre had moved it forward and back and turned and lifted the bucket.

The Jensens hired them both.

Arthur felt pretty good about himself. He watched everything everyone else did and learned quickly. After a while he started thinking he was pretty good.

One time the boss came on the job and Arthur was on the Cat beside a building leveling the ground. He was nervous to see the boss watching and he really didn't know what he was doing because levelling was new to him.

Arthur swung the big front end around and tapped the ground and he saw the boss smile. It made him feel good inside—like he knew what he was doing and the boss was impressed by him—the new guy. Arthur starts to work faster and show off a bit. He went past the building and then turned really quickly and BANG—he hit the building with the bucket.

The boss yanked him off the machine.

At first, he thought he was fired, but he wasn't. He was learning and doing well enough they were willing to look past his mistake. Arthur figured it was because he was good—maybe really good.

A week or so later Arthur went into the office and asked for a raise. Both Jensen brothers were there.

"You want more money, then answer me one question. How do you put oil in the differential?" said one of them

Arthur didn't know.

The two brothers talked it over and one of the brothers went into his office and shut the door.

"No—no raise," said the other one. "In fact, Arthur, we're firing you, so gather up your stuff and go home."

"Okay—I know I'm fired," Arthur said, "but before I go home, could you please tell me where I'd put oil in the differential?"

"No," he said.

"Okay, I just wanted to know." And Arthur walked away.

The brother walked back into his brother's office.

"That Arthur that we fired—there's a guy who is going to get somewhere. He didn't know the answer to the question we asked and after you left, he asked me what the answer was. He's someone who really wants to learn."

Arthur went from one job to another. He never lasted long, but at each job it was always a bigger truck or a bigger tractor, and he took every opportunity to watch and learn.

He applied for a job with a transport company in Winnipeg. When he was asked if he had experience, Arthur said "yeah" and got the job.

On the first day Arthur climbs into the truck cab to go on his first run. It's a tandem truck with two transmissions: one for lower gears, and one for higher gears. Arthur looks at the two sticks and has no clue why there are two sticks.

'Must be a spare, I guess.' He thinks to himself.

He starts it up and grabs one lever, cramming it into gear grinding hard enough to rattle his teeth. It didn't get any easier, every time he shifted it wouldn't be the right RPM and sometimes it was so bad, he had to let go of the shifter. The good thing was, no one could hear it or see that he didn't know what he was doing. As he drove, he started to figure it out and the more he practiced the better he became.

One day the boss tells him to take a run to Portage La Prairie to drive a semi-trailer. Arthur had finally figured out the tandem and now he had to start again with a semi.

"Sure, boss, no problem."

Arthur arrives in Portage La Prairie but he's not allowed to take the semi until he takes a test—he flunks. The guy was mad. Arthur was supposed to already know how to drive a semi.

"I'm a fast learner and I know I could do it if you just gave me a chance and show me."

"Alright," he said. "But without pay."

"Sure," said Arthur, "I'm here for the week, so teach me for the whole week. I'll sleep here, you feed me, and I'll be here all week from morning to night, in that truck, and I'll ride along with different guys." At the end of the week he passed the test.

Arthur kept changing jobs until he finally started to drive graders. But the challenge came when he asked to operate a backhoe. For Arthur it was the biggest challenge. You had to work with a backhoe, not just drive it. Use it like it's connected to your body he was told. Arthur loved the challenge. He learned how to make the hole and tap the bottom nice and smooth.

Arthur felt like he was king, sitting on the backhoe watching the men go into the bottom of the hole he dug to fix a water main or other thing.

"Look, I'm doing my job, you do your job," he used to think.

Then one day he's sitting on the backhoe and they're putting in sewer and water. Arthur's looking at the guys down the hole. And he thinks to myself *'why don't I get myself the heck off my machine and go down the hole and ask them to show me how to set batter boards, how to put fire hydrants, how to tap a main under pressure, how to do a sewer connection, how to set catch basins. And then, I could go on my own. I got a bad attitude sitting up here and not caring what the other guys are doing. Those guys, they are only interested in their paycheque, but me? I'm not interested in my paycheque. I want to be the boss someday.'*

That's when Arthur got a revelation. If he wanted to be the boss one day, he had to learn all there was to know about the business of sewer and water. He had to understand this business inside and out. He looked at people around him and realized that he was not like all the others, he wanted to know everything there was to know about this business. In order to learn, Arthur had to ask questions, find out why things worked the way they did, what machinery did what and how to use it.

Arthur got off his machine and went down the hole and asked the guys, "How do you tap a main under pressure?"

And he kept asking questions on every job, and he learned.

Arthur started a new job one Monday as a backhoe operator. He needed to go to Portage La Prairie and his new boss said his foreman would drive him.

At 6:30 Monday morning, Arthur's foreman, Dave picks him up to take him to the job. Arthur was thrilled. He asked Dave lots of questions and they talked all the way to the jobsite.

Arthur really liked Dave, and it seemed Dave liked him too. Whenever Dave would tell him what to do or explain how to do something, Arthur would concentrate on listening. He never learned in school, and it was so hard for him growing up, to learn to do things and do what he was told. He really wanted to change that.

'I have to listen,' he'd tell himself, *'I have to know what he's saying and remember.'* Arthur started to learn quicker and remember what he learned. He thought about how he learned to control his stutter by concentrating and he was doing the same thing with his job.

"Dave," Arthur said after he'd known him for a while. "Why

don't me and you go into business? You're the foreman—I'm the operator. You know the job and I know how to operate but I don't know enough."

"Yeah, yeah," he said. "We should do that man."

Arthur was 22.

Arthur and Dave kept their plans secret. They kept on working and slowly started to put together their own company. They decided to call it Newdale Construction.

Arthur and Dave became partners. They owned an old ½ ton, red, which Arthur had painted by hand—they nicknamed it the Firebird. Next, they bought a three-ton truck for hauling the pipes—they were all cement pipes and they were heavy. Every morning they hauled the pipes to the job site.

In Arthur's opinion, Dave was a jerk. Perhaps it was because Dave had always showed Arthur things and taught him, so Dave also took on the role as Senior Partner.

Dave started to get on Arthur's nerves. He acted like he knew everything and Arthur didn't know anything—and Arthur was the first one to agree that he didn't know much. But he didn't want to be reminded of it every minute of every day. Arthur clenched his jaw and tried to ignore how mad he was getting and continued to learn.

Arthur decided to hire one of his brothers. He lived out of town and sometimes he'd be 10 minutes late. Dave hated that and would get on his back.

"Your brother's late. We're supposed to start at eight," Dave said to Arthur.

"He's my brother," replied Arthur. "Why don't you let me tell him instead of you?"

But Dave wouldn't. He had to be the boss. He was good, but he was hard to get along with. He and Arthur's brother did not get along at all.

"You are half partner with this guy," his brother would say. "How can you put up with him? Me, you know what? I thought you were different than that. How can you put up with this guy?

Everything you do is wrong, and it's only him that knows, how the heck can you put up?"

Arthur kept his mouth shut, but he knew inside that he put up with it because he was learning. It didn't matter to him if the guy is bad or good. For Arthur it was all about learning.

"Gerry," Arthur said. "I'm learning. I've gotta keep my mouth shut!"

One day, Arthur and Dave drilled a hole through the block of the motor on the backhoe and the oil came out. Arthur knew that Dave wanted to get rid of him and wanted to be on his own, but he didn't want to tell him.

Dave and Arthur were working on a job in East Kildonan pulling pipe across the street. They couldn't dig up the road, so it had to be pushed under it. They had to hire a boring company to do that and there was only one at that time. The boring company used a special patented machine they invented, that dug under the road so the culvert could be pulled through. They worked three hours and charged them $700.

"Dave," said Arthur, "I can make a machine that will do the same thing. Okay—I can build a machine to do that."

"Forget it, you can't do it. Lots of big companies have tried to do it and they have failed. That company holds the patent and they'll sue us and we'll lose our shirts. You can't do it." he said.

'Hmm,' thought Arthur, *'You're going to find out different.'*

The tension between Dave and Arthur got worse. Both of them wanted out, but neither of them would make the first move.

They were hired to do a job in downtown Winnipeg. Arthur's down the hole and needs to try and pull the pipe through. They have the bucket of the machine tied onto a pipe; Arthur put the crow bar in the ground against the bucket and put his arm against the wall. All of a sudden it all let go and his arm went CRACK! Arthur's arm broke. He got up from the ground in shock. He could feel himself getting dizzy. He needed to get out of the hole before he passed out. It's forty below outside and he makes it out of the hole and falls on the ground next to the street.

A police car pulled up. The man working with Arthur tried to talk to him. His eyes were turning in his head and his hands were swelling. By the time the ambulance arrived all the blood on Arthur's clothes was frozen solid.

At the hospital Arthur was given a shot of Novocain to numb the pain. Arthur started feeling strange.

"Doctor," he said, "I'm leaving. I'm dying." The next thing Arthur remembered hearing was— "Okay, his heart is beating and he's breathing again."

Arthur was allergic to the Novocain they gave him and almost died.

With an arm in a cast, Arthur can't work.

"You're no use to the company now. We can barely pay ourselves as it is, if you can't work you can't get paid. Either you buy me out or I'll buy you out—either way we're done."

Arthur sold to him, because he knew that something better was on the horizon. He would tell himself: "If you do what you enjoy, you will do good. And I like what I do."

❧✧☙

Success is not measured by how much money you have It is measured by what you have accomplished.

PART FIVE

THE TRAIL

I crouch again for a minute. Just to stop and hold my breath and listen. If the camp was close then there might be someone there. If I hear them then they might hear me if I yell for help. I hear nothing but the trees. The wind in the frozen trees makes a tinkling sound, almost like a bell. It reminds me of the bells on the cows at home. When it was my job to bring in the cows at night for milking, I'd pray to hear those bells.

We had lots of land, no fences, mostly bush. We had a dog, which loved your Uncle Pierre, but me? Not so much. I wasn't so afraid in the bush with the dog, but the dog didn't always want to go with me.

When I was sent to get the cows from the bush, Papa would sit in his chair and watch me as I left. I could see him looking out the window, sitting in his chair and listening to his radio. I took a stick and listened for the bell and tried to remember which way I was going. It took a long time sometimes to find the cows.

My hands won't warm and if I stay crouched any longer, I won't get up. I start moving forward again—sliding on the frozen ground.

I stop. I think I am going crazy, Son. I've heard of guys who froze to death, but never talked to any who almost froze. My mind, it is playing tricks on me. I look at the trees—the trees are glowing green again and I listen for the cow bells, but there is only the sound of the wind in the trees. I don't know why I'm looking for cows—why I'm looking to hear the bells—I'm not a kid no more.

There it is again. The green light in the trees is moving. It's on the ground in front of me and a little up the trees and its changing colour.

Northern lights are supposed to be in the sky, I didn't think they shine in the trees. And the green light, it moves, Son. And then it disappears and the night is darker than it was before. And I'm alone—except for the panting.

There're clouds in the sky now. Sometimes they drift across the moon and I'm left in darkness. I go around another bend and no camp. I know I've walked more than four miles now. If I had known it was farther than four miles then I would have turned back to the car at two miles. Too late now, though. I can't walk another mile. I am colder than I have ever been, so cold I feel nothing. I am like wood walking. My face is covered with ice and my eyelashes and eyebrows and the bits of hair sticking out from under the toque. I can't bend or crouch down to put my arms around my legs now, I'm too cold. If I tried, I would fall down and stay there in the snow. The first truck to come in the morning would run over me like a lump in the road. So, I keep moving.

I'm certain I hear soft footsteps behind me. I stop. Nothing. I listen harder. I am not alone. I can hear breathing. I hold my breath thinking my ears are playing tricks on me, but I still think I can hear breathing. I turn around slowly, prepared to find myself looking into the dark face of a timber wolf. All I see are trees and bush. I stand still and I listen some more and there it is, only it's not breathing, it's panting. I don't see them, me. I only hear them. They are waiting for me to stop—to lie down so they don't have to chase me. All my life, I have fought the bush—I hate the bush, me, but I love it too. Now the creatures I feared when I was little still wait for me in the dark.

"Stupid Frenchman," I say. "You will have a long wait, you," I say to the wolves. "I am not ready to die. Even if I have to crawl for ten miles you will not get me."

I keep walking, always listening, knowing that death is there for me. If not by the cold, then by a wolf.

I walk faster and as I go I catch sight of another shadow—they are letting me see enough to know I am being followed, eh? And with each clomp of my frozen feet on the frozen snow, and every intake of icy breath, I can feel my body getting colder and my eyes heavier. I don't know how long I've been out here; my hands and my knees burn with daggers of cold digging into my skin. Even warming my hand in my crotch doesn't work anymore.

My eyes, I think they are playing tricks on me now. Is this what happens when someone freezes to death? Do you see things? I look at the trees and sometimes they glow green, almost like flashes of lightening. My heart starts pounding at the thought of lightening. I listen for thunder, but I don't hear it. My mind isn't working, I wonder, can there be lightning and thunder in the winter when there is only a small puff of clouds?

I was afraid of the bush as a kid and scared of the bears and wolves, but okay, I was terrified of the lightning. I'd see a flash and my breathing would stop, my eyes wide, and I'd wait to see how close the lightning was. Then, when it was far away, there would be the low grumble of thunder and I'd breath, walk quicker, and pray I would find the cows quickly. Another flash, and the land around me would jump to brightness without shadows and I would feel the panic hit my throat. Crack! And the thunder boomed and I knew it was close. Maybe catching a tree on fire and I would be lost in the bush with a prairie fire raging towards me at the speed of a freight train. In a panic I would run when I see the flash of lightening and then I'd have to stop and take some breaths and make myself calm down. No matter what I couldn't go home without the cows. If I did Papa would take off his belt and bellow how stupid I was. I was so terrified of Papa and his belt, I'd pee myself, soon. And Papa, sure he hit me in the head sometimes and I learned to duck whenever I passed him, but when he was mad and he kept hitting and hitting and hitting. Okay, that was real terror then.

So, I ran in the lightning and the thunder and the wind and the torrential downpour in the blackness of a prairie thunderstorm trying to listen for the bells on the cows—I'd pray as I ran. Then —far off to my right I heard it. A tinkle of a bell between the roar of the thunder. —the cows—I found them!

I don't care now; I need to drink. I scoop up some snow and melt it in my mouth before swallowing. I feel the sting on the inside of my mouth, but the water? Okay, it feels good.

A shadow crosses the road about thirty feet in front of me and I hear low growling off to the right. I don't see no timber wolves much these days, since I left home. And only then in the winter when they are really hungry and they smell Mama's chickens. I strain my eyes, trying to see where and how many there are but it's no use. Wolves are the ghosts of the prairies, if you're close enough to see 'em, then you're too close. Ah me. I am in much trouble now.

I sweat, yet I freeze. It all feels like a dream and sometimes, I almost feel warm, but then I'm cold again. I'm colder than when there was a blizzard and we were all stuck inside the house. The wind would rattle and rattle everything that was loose and the stove couldn't keep the cold away. Do you remember, Son? In the first house Papa built—wait—I was the boy; you weren't born yet. I'm getting muddled.

In the winter, it was the snow storms and the cold we battled against. In the summer it was the bugs, the heat, thunderstorms and tornados.

I'm thinking they are going to find me dead on the road because I am hallucinating. The green lights look exactly like the northern lights. That's what they look like. The light is green and moving in the trees and I'm thinking this is it, no noise, no nothing, I'm hallucinating, I'm freezing and this is it, I'm done for.

I keep on walking and you see I'm worried about them cutting off my legs if someone finds me before I'm really dead. You see, I'm so cold, I don't know at what point they cut off my legs, you see, I don't know that.

No noise, no nothing. My legs are like a pinching and I'm going on my knees and I'm not moving and I don't feel my feet but my legs, they are hurting and it's hard walking and I'm seeing the lights and I'm wondering is this what happens before death? Maybe there are lights before you die? I struggle to my feet—if I stay down the wolves…

I have had problems with me today, with claustrophobia. Because my brother molested me. People forget that if you abuse a child, they think the child is little and cannot defend himself—they are not going to stay like that, children. They get by and punch your clock maybe—one of those days maybe. Because of that I got claustrophobia with elevators, with closets. And in construction I made tunnels under the ground and I would have to get out to secure myself. I had to secure myself and say "Hey, it's shored. It's okay. I got shoring and nothing's going to happen." So, then I could go back. Until then I had to get out, prove that I could get out and then it was okay to go back. And today, I still got phobia. But I have overcome it like on elevators for example. I still got the phobia, but I will still go in the elevator. I'll face my problem and I always want to better myself.

I'm standing on the road and I'm looking at the sky and it's clear, and so cold. What the heck am I going to do? And I say,

"Lord you said that if I go into…. I didn't go out on purpose to come out here, but somehow you would rescue me from things. I don't know what you can do, I mean I have all the tools in my mind on how to survive, but I'm stuck and I mean business, and I keep seeing those things move around in the trees. It's Sunday night, I know nobody's coming and the camp is not here and I will die. Nobody will find me until morning. I know that—the road is closed; nobody is going to come."

Arthur and his children.

CHAPTER TWENTY-EIGHT

DEER HUNTING IN WINNIPEG

Arthur's cousin, Gilbert, was dating a very pretty blonde girl named Lorraine. Arthur loved blondes, even when he was little. Arthur's brothers teased him about Lorraine and told him he should try to take her away from Gilbert. When Arthur met her, he felt an instant attraction. It looked like she was attracted to him as well, so Arthur poured on as much charm as he could. Arthur and Lorraine started to date right after she broke up with Gilbert.

Arthur was 18 when Lorraine told him she was pregnant.

There were few choices back then for pregnant girls. Lorraine's mother pushed for the two of them to get married. That scared Arthur. He was young and didn't make enough money to support a family. But that didn't change the fact that he was as responsible as Lorraine and he had to deal with it—besides, he loved kids and was excited about being a dad.

Lorraine and Arthur were married on May 22, 1968. The birth of his son was the happiest moment of Arthur's life. Holding that little baby in his arms he promised he would always love him. He thought for sure that his son would be the cutest baby in the nursery. What he didn't know was that many times the doctors will use forceps to help with the birth and that it causes the head to be slightly slanted at the beginning. When Arthur first saw his son, he said to himself: 'He's got a head like a clawhammer" – Fortunately, his son turned out to be a beautiful baby after all, to Arthur's relief.

At first the couple lived with Lorraine's mom and dad and that did not work. Arthur started making better money and they moved into their own place. They lived for a while where Arthur acted as the caretaker, so the rent was lower and he received $15 a month for looking after the place. They had two more kids, and Arthur loved his kids. He loved them like crazy.

At 23 years old Arthur is hunting with a thirteen-year-old kid named Alfred and another guy on Wilkes Avenue in Winnipeg. It was against the law to shoot a gun inside the city limits. Arthur's on Wilkes Avenue shooting deer. They killed four or 5 deer and skinned them and brought the meat home.

One night they decide to go hunting and parked the car on Wilkes. They walk along the bush trails about a half mile and they see a herd of deer in the field—about 50 of them. They were too far to shoot them, so they started to sneak closer. Suddenly something spooks them and they all take off running straight towards Arthur and his friends.

"There's somebody there," Arthur tells the others.

The three of them run back to the car. The others go home and Arthur goes downtown to a coffee shop. He doesn't want to go home. He's got a funny feeling. The next morning, he calls home.

"The cops came here asking for you," Lorraine told him.

The police hadn't told her anything, just that they wanted to talk to Arthur. He called her back about an hour later and she says "you better come home, there are cops all over the place."

Arthur drives home in his truck. He's thinking of every question the police might ask him and he's trying to think of the right answer to make them go away. The police didn't know that the kids were with him. The police were waiting for him.

"You are Arthur?" They asked.

"Yeah,"

"You've been hunting on Wilkes?"

"No. I haven't been hunting on Wilkes. Why?"

"You've been hunting deer."

Arthur realizes the police saw him and had taken down the license number of his car—that's how they found him.

He said, "Hold on a minute. What do you mean you weren't there?"

"You asked me if I was hunting on Wilkes—I wasn't hunting on Wilkes."

"Can you tell me what your car was doing on Wilkes?"

"Was it on Wilkes? I don't know what it was doing on Wilkes, I didn't take it there."

"Oh, so you saying your car drove itself?"

"No, the car doesn't drive by itself, but I didn't take it there. If you say it was there, then I believe you that you saw it there. I didn't take it there."

"Who did you lend your car to?"

"Alan Anderson."

"Where does he live?"

"I don't know."

"Oh, so you lend your car to people you don't know?"

"No. I know him—I just don't know where he lives. He came here to borrow my car, I loaned it to him. And he took off with my car. I don't know where he went."

"Your car is going to be impounded or seized."

"You do what you have to do. I'm telling you I did not hunt on Wilkes."

Arthur knows he's got one piece of venison in his freezer. The freezer is big enough to put the couch in there and there's one piece of meat right at the bottom. He's a bit worried and starts to wonder.... *Will Lorraine think to take that one piece of venison and get rid of it? No,'* He thought to himself, *'she won't think of it.'* Arthur starts to figure a way to explain the deer meat in his freezer.

"Ok, Arthur." The cops say. "Open the trunk of your car."

He does as he's asked. It's full of blood, and bullets. One police officer picks up a bullet and looks at his partner and says "we got him."

"So, what's all the blood in there?"

"I killed some chickens."

"You show me some chicken that bleeds like that and I'll buy it."

"Well, I don't care what you gonna say."

"Your wife—you been hunting on Wilkes and you're a liar, and your wife knows you're a liar and your wife, she doesn't want to fink on you."

"What do you mean she doesn't want to fink on me?"

"I asked your wife where you were and she said she didn't want to fink on her husband."

"Let me tell you something. Before someone can fink on you, they got to know something about you. My wife? I know she knows nothing so I know she cannot fink. My wife doesn't know where I go or what I do so I know she cannot fink on me."

"Well, we know you've been hunting on Wilkes Road."

"Well, if you know that then you charge me. But you don't know nothing and the reason you're asking me questions is because you don't know nothing. If you know something you don't ask, you charge."

Arthur finds Lorraine, "you go to church and you pray, and you leave me here to babysit because then they can't take me to the police station and they can't charge me—get outta here, go pray." She was going to church anyway. She was only hanging around because the police were there.

Arthur knew he had to be careful what he said and not to say too much. He didn't want to get caught lying because they would really get tough.

"So, do you have any deer meat in your house?"

"Yeah, yeah I do."

"Oh," he says, "that's good."

"Yeah, it is good. I like deer meat, it's very good. It's just one piece of meat."

"So, where does that come from?"

"Do you know where St. Labre, Manitoba is?"

He says, "Yeah."

"I was in St. Labre, Manitoba and there's this road called the 31, and that road goes all the way to the TransCanada Highway. When I got to the TransCanada Highway there was this man having trouble with his car," Arthur knows he's lying but he doesn't care. "And he's having trouble with his car and I stopped to help him and he thanked me and asked me if I wanted a piece of deer meat. Well, I like deer meat, so I says yeah."

Arthur knew that the deer meat wouldn't match any deer in Winnipeg because it was from a deer he killed in St. Labre. But what he was scared of was all the deer carcasses he threw into the garbage—they belonged to the deer from Wilkes road. The officer seemed to read his mind and they searched the garbage. What Arthur didn't know was the garbage had been hauled away hours ago. The police found nothing.

"Okay," says the police when Arthur gives them the deer meat from the freezer, "you have to come to the police station with us."

"I can't," said Arthur. "My wife has gone to church and my kids are asleep in the house. I can't leave them, I'm babysitting. I'm not going nowhere."

"Yes, you are. You have to come to the police station with us."

"No, I'm not. You got nothing if you do then you charge me. But I'm not going with you."

"Well," he says. "Can I use your phone?"

"Sure."

He calls the sheriff. "What are we going to do with this guy?"

So, the sheriff came and he asked Arthur to tell him what he told the Police. Arthur repeated every word.

"So," the sheriff says to Arthur. "I'll tell you what. I've got this piece of meat here; if it matches the deer from Wilkes Road then we'll be back."

"Well," Arthur replies, "you know what? Bon voyage! You won't come back then, because it won't match."

The police took the deer meat and charged Arthur $15 for possessing deer meat out of season. He paid the fine and never heard from them again.

❧ ❖ ☙

**Be proud of your accomplishments
and your failures – each has brought you experience.**

CHAPTER TWENTY-NINE

A HARD LESSON

After selling out to Dave, Arthur decided to start a new company with a new partner. He and his partner Wayne started Atlas Utilities Contractors.

Wayne was a qualified engineer. Arthur was so impressed and excited. He had come a long way since he left St. Labre. He was a business man, was making money, and learning so much that an engineer actually wanted him as a partner. He grew up thinking he was ugly and stupid—he was neither. Girls liked him—a lot, and he had educated people who thought he was smart.

Arthur looked back at the days when he took the abuse and kept his mouth shut so he could learn as much as he could. He wasn't finished learning, but maybe he didn't have to take the garbage as much.

Wayne was really good at bidding for jobs, and Arthur did some bidding as well but Adam did most of the hands-on work.

Arthur was busy doing a job to put down 12 miles of water line out of town, and Wayne was overseeing the smaller job in town at the same time—a drainage ditch. Arthur had been busy all week and he hadn't had a chance to look at Wayne's project. Wayne told him the job was done and sent Arthur to go pick up the cheque from the customers.

He went into the office and asked the customer if the cheque was ready for Atlas.

"The job is finished," said the man in the office. "But it's not right, it's backwards—it's flowing the wrong way."

"I don't understand that," said Arthur. "What do you mean?"

Wayne had done the job so the water drained from catch basin to catch basin. But he sent it in the wrong direction. It was pooling at the start of the drainage ditch instead of draining away.

"Unless you fix it," the customer said, "there'll be no cheque."

Arthur went to town to take a look and to get it fixed so they could get paid. He looked at the bid Wayne had made on the job. It should have been cost plus so fixing it should have cost the customer more. Usually, when you run into something that is not in the contract, then you stop the job and go to the engineer and say this is not part of the deal, this is not part of the contract, not on the blueprint, there's something wrong in your blueprint and you didn't account for it. The general contractor has to say go ahead, they haven't a choice, but they still have to give the okay for us to proceed. Wayne didn't do that. He continued and finished the job without talking to the General Contractor.

The job had to be fixed. It meant doing the job twice for half the money at Atlas Utilities Contractors' expense.

The company was dissolved. Wayne and Arthur both struggled against bankruptcy. All the equipment was sold to pay bills, even though Arthur wanted to keep one machine and truck so he could continue to make a living. He was back at the beginning. He found starting over was harder than anything he had ever done.

To top it off, Wayne sold the last equipment that Arthur had kept and he was stuck with nothing at all. He had to start anew from scratch. It took him five years before he could get over it.

❧❖☙

What you believe shapes who you become.

CHAPTER THIRTY

STARTING OVER

Arthur lost almost everything, and he still owed money to Supercrete. "Look," Arthur said to the people at Supercrete, "I was in business with this guy—he's an engineer—a qualified engineer. I thought he knew what he was doing, I trusted him and me, well I was doing okay before, I still know what I know and I can get back there. I'm not giving up; I can still do the work and I need to recover. But he's got me into the hole so far, I can't see my way out."

"I want to pay you. I know I owe you, but I can't pay you the whole thing. Can we negotiate a price?"

"Arthur," they said to him. You were doing okay on your own, we don't know why you hooked up with a partner. We'll need to get the partners together and talk about it and we'll let you know."

Arthur's friend Gabriel is a part owner of Supercrete. (Gabriel was the man that helped Arthur get back to St. Labre when his sister was lost in the bush.) He gets all the partners together.

"I know Arthur." Gabriel told them. "He's a good person even though he's young. He's smart and has overcome amazing obstacles and was on the right road. How he got mixed up with this engineer guy I don't know, but he did really well on his own. Then he goes into this partnership and he loses everything. He came in here to work out a deal and didn't just stick us with the cost and skip town. That says something about his character and his business sense. I think we should help him out."

Arthur and the partners of Supercrete compromised on the bill, and Arthur paid them.

Arthur realized too, that Gabriel had influence with the company and he knew Gabriel had put his own reputation on the line with the partners, to give Arthur a chance.

Paying off his debts wasn't the only thing Arthur struggled with. He needed to rebuild his business. He could bid and get jobs, but he needed the money for material and wages before he'd see any money from the jobs. By renegotiating with Supercrete he was able to keep a small amount for start-up costs, but he had to be smart with it to make it do what he needed.

Arthur got a job and he needed hubs for the main. He goes to Supercrete to buy what he needs. This company, they are a multi-million-dollar outfit, and they have pipes all over the yard. The average price of the pipe was $6.50 per length.

Some of the pipes were cracked pipes during shipping or loading and the company kept them separated from the good ones. They weren't broken, just cracked; they were still usable.

Arthur walks over to the pile of cracked pipes and looks at them carefully. The cracks were really tiny.

'Hm,' He thought to himself, *'if I buy the hubs here, I wonder if they'd let me have those pipes too— really cheap?'*

"Gabriel," said Arthur, "I need the hubs on the main to do my connection, could you let me have the cracked pipes for a better deal."

"Yeah, sure Arthur, I'll give them to you for .25 each."

Arthur walks back out to the yard with a spring in his step.

"Hey," he says to the yard supervisor. "Load me up with all those pipes."

"I can't do that," he says. "Those are cracked, we can't sell them."

"You can to me; Gabriel said I could have them." The supervisor still didn't believe him and went into the office to check. He came out without saying a word and loaded up Arthur's truck.

Arthur started Adam's Underground at the age of 26.

❧❖❦

Always think long-term. Be excited.

Arthur's invention.

CHAPTER THIRTY-ONE

THE PATENT

After selling his half of Newdale Construction, Arthur started to invent his patent, the boring machine that Dave said he couldn't build, in his spare time. When he lost everything with Atlas, Arthur started focusing on his invention seriously.

As he works on his own, it gives him lots of time to think. In the back of his mind he's thinking of the issues and problems around shooting a machine under a road so culverts or pipes can be pushed through without tearing up the road.

"Hey," he calls his brother one night. "You not too busy you, pushing pipe? I hear you're quitting. You want to sell me your stuff so I can push pipe?"

"Yeah, I'll even show you how to do it."

His brother sold him the truck and equipment for $500 and went on one job with him to show him how to do it.

"You put the frame down, line it up, put the level on it and shoot to the other hole."

Arthur was on his own. He gets to the job and he has a 200lb metal frame on the back of the truck. On his own he manages to unload it, and pushes it down into the hole. He's in water up to his knees, and he's trying to get everything level so he can shoot across, but everything is lifting up and he's having a lot of problems. Once done, he has to remove it by hand. He struggles all morning.

At 12 o'clock he looks around and sees a guy standing around, "Can you pass me that piece of wood?"

"Oh, no, we're going for lunch," he says.

Arthur can't believe that the guy couldn't even pass him a piece of wood. He crawls out of the hole, and grabs the piece of wood to level things up. The wood is floating and won't stay in place and Arthur is swearing and can't believe the trouble he's having.

On the way home that night, Arthur thinks about the problems on the job. He had to find a way to anchor the frame so it wouldn't shift with water.

He went into his garage and welded long pieces of square steel along the edge of the frame. He drilled holes in it next, so he could pound metal rods through the holes into the ground when he was ready to anchor it. That way he could use jacks in the front for shoring and boards to level it and then he can tighten the frame so when he shoots it doesn't lift.

He tried it on the job site and it worked like a dream.

Every job had different problems. Every night Arthur would go into his garage after work and find solutions to the problems.

Arthur won a bid for a job with the Water Service Board—a government job—good pay. Arthur made a plan. *This is what I'm going to do. If I can work one month out of the year, I'll make more money than if I worked at something else or for another company for a full year.*

Arthur started getting more and more jobs. Up to that point, there was only one company who pushed culverts, water and sewer lines and copper lines. They had a special machine for shooting under the road, and Arthur was taking their jobs.

A registered letter is sent to Arthur Adam, of Adam's Underground. He had his wife read it to him. No matter how much he learned, even learned to speak English, he couldn't seem to learn to read or write.

"You have been doing work underground and we want you to

cease and desist using all equipment that would infringe on our patents".

The patent numbers were listed at the bottom of the letter. Giving Arthur that information was a big mistake.

Arthur always believed he didn't know anything—which is why he wanted to learn. He sat down and talked to himself in order to figure it out.

"This guy has 19 trucks," He said, "a big office—and I'm a nobody—I'm a kid, I'm only 25 years old. Wait a minute—what is this guy scared of? I'm nothing! He must be worried about me, to send me stuff like that."

Arthur had an epiphany. The other company woke up a slumbering giant.

Arthur had someone help him to look up the patent numbers on the letter. He wanted to see what the other company had. He looks at their apparatus and the method. He studied their patent and Arthur build a different machine that was better and more efficient than theirs.

"Hey," He called his brother. "I need some scraps of metal. You give me some?"

Arthur welded his own boring machine in his garage. He made it with everything the existing machine didn't have like: broaching head with doors in it, a rotating shooting rod with fins so when it hits a rock it will be harder to push it off course, the fins will unscrew to make it easier to retract the rod. The doors on Arthur's boring machine will close when it gets pulled back so all the dirt comes out with it.

The hardest thing he ever had to do when inventing his boring machine, was keeping quiet until he got his patent.

While he waited, he stopped working as Adam Underground and leaves the province. He took a job as the supervisor of the Eldorado Gold mine in Ontario. The other company thought their letter worked, and he was able to earn enough for his family still in Winnipeg.

When he was notified that his patent was protected, he returned to Winnipeg. The first thing he did was call his ex-partner Dave.

Dave walked around Arthur's machine, which he had in his garage. He looked at it from every angle, and Arthur waits for him to say something. Dave didn't say a word. He left the garage, got into his truck and sped off.

Arthur had told Dave he could build a better machine and if he'd believed him, he could have had half. Arthur learned so much from him. But he missed his chance.

As well, Arthur was the only company that won a lawsuit against the competition because he had his own patent that was a new device and did not infringe on their patent.

Many people think of new ideas, while working with equipment or tools they work with every day. If you want to create a patent, you must be prepared. You have to prepare a good presentation, with diagrams, if necessary, and you must know your subject matter thoroughly. You have to be ready for any question they will ask you. Any new idea can become a reason to claim for a patent.

❧❖☙

You only have one name, don't ruin it.

CHAPTER THIRTY-TWO

LEVELING OUT THE PLAYING FIELD

Arthur knows how good his machine is. He knows it's worth a lot of money— but he doesn't know how to take the next step.

Arthur takes it to Jensen Brothers, the guys he worked for 10 years earlier.

"I made this," he said to them showing them his machine. "Its patent pending and I want to know if you'll give me work. Okay—I'd give you a good deal. We could make a heck of a lot of money with this thing."

"Well, for sure we'll give you work. This is unbelievable what you got here." They said to him. "There's big money in that. Do you know how much we pay to the other company every year? And that's just us. Everybody has to use them and they charge what they want because there is no competition—until now. We wish you good luck and we're very happy for you."

'Okay,' Arthur thought to himself, *'They don't want to make tons of cash. I'll have to think about who else to take it to.'* He got into his truck and went home. He heard the phone ringing the minute he walked in the door.

"Allo."

"We need to talk to you," it was the Jensen brothers "Can you come back?"

"Can we become your partner?" They asked him when he got there. It felt pretty good to hear that, but Arthur was careful not to seem too excited. He needed to put on a bargaining face— a poker face.

"How much would you charge us for the rights of half of Manitoba?" he said to Arthur.

"Well, what would you give me?" Said Arthur. He was in a dream—he never had any money and here these rich guys—richer than Arthur ever thought he could ever be—wanted to give him money for something he created out of his head.

'Maybe, I'm not so stupid.' He thought.

"I'll tell you what," they said, "We'll give you $50,000."

'Wow…' thought Arthur. *'$50,000! I grew up with nothing—still got nothing. I never felt important, I thought I was stupid. I had nothing going for me. Right now, I don't even have a dime in my pocket—$50,000.'* On the inside his heart was racing at the thought of it, but on the outside— nothing.

'If they offer me that right off, maybe they are starting low. I saw something in their faces that told me that when they looked at my machine, their mouths watered. They want it bad. I don't know what half of the rights to Manitoba are worth, but I bet it's worth more than that.'

"Oh—no," Arthur said. "No way—it's worth much more than that." Arthur was living a dream.

"Well, how much do you want?"

"At least ……….. I need a lot more than that, this is a big deal, and if the other company decides to fight me, you pay the lawyer's bill."

"Get the cheque book," he says to his brother, "We got a deal."

Manitoba alone did millions back then of underground work which meant a lot of money. Arthur sold half for an undisclosed amount of money. To Arthur it was a fortune and yet, the first thing he thought was maybe he didn't ask for enough. Yet, what he received was more than a dollar amount. He was given credibility by two well respected businessmen.

The next battle started with talking to Ottawa, patent lawyers, and jumping through hoops that cost Arthur more than he had at the time. Then, the other company with their boring machine, decided to start a war.

One day a guy walks into Arthur's shop.

"Are you Arthur Adam?" he asked.

"Yeah, I am."

"Now, don't get mad at me. I'm only here to give you this message. The business you're in is not worth it. Get out of it before somebody hurts you—or worse."

"Really?" said Arthur. "That guy who sent you to give me that message? You go tell that guy, that I come from a family of nineteen kids. I got thirteen brothers, and when my dad gave me a licking, it was with an axe. So, you go tell him I'm not scared of him or anything he thinks he can do to me. He'll never stop me. If he takes me on then he's gonna get the whole family—him. Okay—tell him he'd better get out of my face."

One day Arthur was doing a shot on Waverly, in Winnipeg. He had to line it up and shoot the machine over to the other side into a little hole under the road. And it was bang on. He came out of the hole and a man is sitting there in his Lincoln watching him. Arthur suspected it was the owner of the other company.

Arthur gets back into the hole to shoot under the road to another hole a long way away. He knew the man was watching and Arthur decided to show off. The shot was dead on.

"Where did you learn to do that?" he said to Arthur. "You need to come work for me."

"I don't work for cheap outfits," said Arthur.

"I want to tell you something and you better listen to me, Arthur. Get out of my farmyard."

"No, you get out of mine."

"Look, you don't know who you're talking to. I have never lost a fight—physical, or in court—I have never lost a fight."

"Don't you talk like that," said Arthur. "You're gonna lose a fight really quick and it's one that will happen right now. You will never stop me. Do you understand? You can try and stop me here or I'll come out over there."

"Why don't you go to Ontario to push?"

"Why don't you go to Ontario to push? I'm staying right here."

He left.

So, little Arthur, the kid who grew up with no toilet, 9 pairs of shoes between 13 kids, eating scraps of bread he stole from the family dog or out of the school garbage can. With a grade 2 education, he now had a business and an invention and more work than he could handle. And this thing, it wasn't like the mom and pop corner store. His shop was Canada and the US to start with. Soon he started receiving calls from other countries. Arthur—the ugly Adam kid who couldn't read or write.

Next, the other company contacted Arthur's patent lawyer in Winnipeg and told him he was in conflict of interest and he had to quit doing legal work for Adam's Underground.

"You know what?" Arthur's lawyer told them. "If it is a conflict of interest, then I can't do your legal work either."

Arthur had to go to Ottawa to find a good patent lawyer. A few weeks later the Patent Attorneys arrived in Winnipeg for a meeting.

There were quite a few people, sitting around the conference table at the Winnipeg Inn. There were two patent attorneys from Ottawa, a secretary and 25-year-old Arthur Adam, plus quite a few contractors who would have loved to get their hands on such an important device that each and every one wanted. The patent attorneys are addressing their comments and questions directly to Arthur. If someone at the table interrupted, they would still return back to Arthur for clarity. It suddenly hit Arthur. All those people were there because of him.

'Hey! I'm not stupid.' He realized.

**Never underestimate your inner self.
If it feels good, do it!**

PART SIX

THE TRAIL

I am scared—terrified—exhausted. I'm done. I can't move my feet no more, so I don't even try. It's all I can do to stay standing.

I want to sink to my knees, Son, lie down in the snow and close my eyes; but the lights; the green lights. They are running around the trees and making my shadow look so tall. They are getting brighter and changing colour. I can see the bark on the trees and every tire print on the trail ahead . . .

I know I'm going to die, unless a miracle took place. I know I am facing death. I know I'm going to die.

"God!" I tried to yell out, but the sound came like a rasp. I couldn't cry, because my tears are frozen. "God!" I called out again and this time the word came out. "Lord! Save me. Lord Help Me!"

I turn around and I see headlights. They are getting brighter, getting closer—almost blinding me. I stand and watch, not sure if I'm dreaming.

Did I lie down in the snow Son? Am I lying on the ground and dreaming as my life is leaving my body? Are there really lights? Or am I imagining again?

It's not a dream. I'm in the middle of the road and a truck is coming towards me real slow-like.

I don't care if he runs me over. This guy can kill me, Son. I'm not moving out of the way. This truck is not getting past me—I know I'm finished if he leaves me here.

I hold my ground and watch the truck move to me in slow motion.

I know the guy driving that truck must be scared like hell, Son. When you see a frozen man in the road standing up—you don't want to pick up a monster in the road. He don't know me. I wouldn't blame any man for not stopping. I mean—I'm full of frost—covered in white. I'm an ice-man, me.

I stay where I am and wait.

Am I going to die under his tires? Do I die in the snow? Does he stop and save me? Please God. I want to see my kids; hold them, love them like never before. Let him stop.

He's getting closer and I'm watching him get closer and I don't move until the truck stops.

I can't believe it, Son. I mean, the truck, its right in front of me and it's not moving. What a miracle! I can't let him drive away.

I walk right down the middle of the road towards the truck so he can't pass.

If the driver gets spooked and tries to drive away, I'm going to jump on the truck. I'll hang on and ride on the hood until he stops and lets me in or we get to wherever he is going. He's not getting past me . . . God! He's not leaving me here!

I get right up to the truck. I see the shadow of the man behind the wheel, but it is too dark to look into his eyes. I stare right where I think his eyes are. I look right there as I lean over and plant both my hands on the hood.

Don't drive away, mister. Please. Let me get inside where it's warm.

Keeping my hands on the truck I walk like a crab on frozen feet around the side and grab at the door handle. My fingers don't want to work and I feel the emotion build in me. I keep grabbing and finally, the door opens.

Okay—I am happy, me. I see my brother, Leo, sitting next to the driver.

Son, Papa is coming home . . .

THE FINAL WORD

Many people who have read my first book, ask me to explain how I became a millionaire. How does a little boy from the country, without any education, who knew nothing, could become a millionaire with no role model to follow? A lot of people still do not believe me. They think I am pulling the wool over their eyes, that I am lying, or that I make believe that I am rich when I am not. To resume all my life, I would need another book. The only thing I can say is that I worked hard, probably harder than many educated people because I could not read or write properly. I had to learn from memory, most of the time, everything that was taught to me. I've always had a hunger to learn, anything, anytime, however important it was or not at the time. Everything was interesting to me. I was like a sponge absorbing everything in my memory. And I was fortunate to have a good memory. That was my first talent, I think. Then, my second talent, was that I was persistent. I did not quit a job half done, it had to be done to perfection. And I was adamant about that.

I also quickly learned that to make money in this country of ours, you are better off working for yourself, rather than to work for other people. When you are self-employed and you are your own boss, you have deductions for your tools, your trucks, your tractors, meals, taxes and many other deductions that a good accountant can tell you about. On top of that, his expenses are deductible too!

And you must be creative. I never shied away from work - the harder the job the better. I called them "specialty jobs" where nobody wanted to take them on. That is what payed the most, when no one else will do it, you can charge more. You have free rein. But be prepared to work hard.

At first, I would repair sewer connections, etc. I did not own any kind of fancy machinery, other than my truck and a shovel, unlike the big competitors who had machinery to do the heavy work. One day, in the beginning, I met this lady who was looking for a plumber to fix her sewer problem. I told her I worked on sewers but I was not a plumber. She agreed to hire me for a set rate we had agreed upon. When I got to her place, the sewer was located in between two houses, hers and her neighbor's. No machinery would have been able to get in there, even if I had had the equipment. I started to dig by hand, eight feet deep to get to the broken sewer. I quickly discovered that the sewer served two houses and that the neighbor's sewer was backing up in my client's house. I waited until late afternoon and when the neighbor came home, I quickly explained the situation to him and after much discussion, he agreed to pay half of the cost to repair this sewer pipe. It ended costing more but divided into both neighbors, my customer ended up having to pay less than originally agreed. She was happy and I went home with more money than originally requested. Persistence paid off in that instance.

I quickly learned too that a good accountant is not a luxury. It is a necessity. They can give you good advice, help direct you and keep you from making major mistakes in the world of finances. You can't know it all, about everything, especially if you are an uneducated kid like I was. What you need is more common sense.

Once I got serious about working in the sewer business, I bought myself a truck and a backhoe to dig the trenches. After a while, watching over my money, I paid off my first machine, bought a second one and after a while, paid that one off too. That was the way I operated. Don't spend more than you make, go over your means. Again, use common sense.

One day, I received a call from a man who wanted to hire me to repair a problem he had with his sewer line. I quoted him a certain amount, and proceeded to his apartment block. When I got there, the problem was way more than what he had told me. Two plumbers were standing at the door of a crawl space, under the apartment block and neither of them would touch this job. When I looked in the crawl space, I couldn't believe my eyes. There, before me, was a crawl space full of raw sewage, four feet deep and the length of the apartment block. Of course, the owner of the premises did not want to contact the city engineers – that would have meant putting all his tenants in hotel rooms for a few nights until the problem was fixed. I looked the problem over and realized that I could repair the damage by doing what I called a "by-pass" in the sewage system and quickly got to work. Within eight hours, with my equipment, I dug under the apartment block, found the main sewer line and performed a "by-pass" that permitted all the sewage to drain out of the crawl space to the city's main sewer. Then, the plumbers finished the job. Before beginning the work, I made sure the price was bumped up and I went home that night with a substantial amount of money for one day's work.

I also learned that you have to know how to bid on contracts, which I learned by listening and looking at others bidding on jobs to see how they did it. Each contractor, each banker, each business man I met would teach me something. I had a dream of becoming a millionaire. With determination, courage and persistence, you can accomplish what I did. When I bid on a job, I took into consideration the time it would take, the salary of the men and the equipment I would need, the material involved and added 20%. I also watched the body language – when bidding on contracts. That usually told me if the bid was too high or too low. It did not come easy. I put a lot of blood, sweat and tears in all the projects I accomplished. I worked both physically and mentally. I've had disappointments, and setbacks. All business people can expect that. But, each time, I looked at it as a lesson learned for next time.

Of course, luck has had a lot to do with my success. I never made quick on the spot decisions. I always weighed the pros and cons before making a decision about a contract. I've always treated others the way I would like to be treated. My word is sacred. I honor my work and expect others to do the same. It is very important to build an honorable reputation. As they say, your reputation precedes you. In the business world, and in my business world especially, you have to honor your word. If you can't meet the expectations set out in your contract, face it and negotiate some other arrangement to everybody's satisfaction. Do not hide from your responsibilities. Do not expect people to do things for free.

I've learned that to make money you have to have money. But it was a challenge to find the money to start. That was the real challenge. You can do it, if you have a vision, a dream, that you don't lose along the way. Use your head and watch your money!

I have to admit that I have a "business sense" that many educated people do not have and will never have. It may be a gift, a talent, or it could be from the way I was raised. In my family, you had to fend for yourself, forge ahead if you wanted something, learn to keep out of trouble, and if you did get in trouble, find a way to get out of it by yourself. All my youth I spent doing that. I could have felt sorry for myself, but I did not. I never had the love of a mother, the advice of a father, the joy of growing up in a loving family but I got myself out of it. If you are reading this book, and find yourself in a similar situation, do not despair. Patience, courage and the help of God will bring you the success you deserve. Just set your vision and forge ahead!

An extraordinary experience:
Once his patent was recognized and approved, two men

approached Arthur to purchase half the rights to his patent for Canada and the US. The two men were reliable and solvent. Arthur accepted to deal with them. Their proposal was to give a certain amount as down payment, now, and the balance in one year. They had both put their own residences as collateral to seal the deal. Unfortunately, the deal they were making on their end turned sour and they had to declare bankruptcy. Arthur, on the advice of his lawyer, was told to sue them. Arthur decided to meet them instead before proceeding to such dramatic measures.

When he was seated across from them, he asked:

"What would you do, if you were me?"

They were hesitant to answer, of course. Finally, one of them said: "I would go for the agreement that we signed originally." That meant that both business men would lose their homes. Arthur thought long and hard about the whole situation and finally decided to let the matter go and not sue them, although that meant losing a great deal of money.

Some seven years later, a businessman offered a huge amount of money to Arthur for shares in his patent. He gave a large deposit and promised to come up with the difference in one month. One morning, a few days before the end of the month when the agreement would become due, the man appeared on Arthur's doorstep, feeling very sheepish, and reported to Arthur that the firm for which he practiced saw the deal with Arthur as a conflict of interest and he would have to retire from the agreement with Arthur. However, he was leaving the deposit and did not want to be refunded for it. It was the exact same amount that Arthur had forgiven to the two businessmen who had put their personal homes up for collateral, some years earlier. That is God's work.

❧ ❖ ☙

**Never fear having to pass another test,
Win another verdict, sign another agreement,
It is what makes you a winner!**

Following in Grandpa's footsteps, *The Trail* is very different for Arthur's family.

ABOUT THE AUTHOR

Adam lives in Steinbach, Manitoba. He spends his time singing country songs, picking tunes on his guitar, and has even recorded several music CDs with his friends. He collects antique cars and if there is a car show around, he will most likely be there. Adam is a pastor/evangelist at heart and his greatest joy comes from talking to people about the Lord. There is a famine in the land today, not of water or of bread, but of hearing the Word of God. He and his wife, Edie, are always looking for people to talk to and opportunities to share with others the goodness and truth of God. When they aren't at Shiloh, they spend much of their time between Canada and the United States forging relationships and witnessing to those who are searching.

They plan on visiting churches across North America in the future to share their story and their hope in the one true God.

To invite Adam to your church or organization
Email adamedith5599@gmail.com for more information or
Call Adam 204-392-6767

Made in the USA
Middletown, DE
07 July 2023